FROM
THE
EARTH

Dear Ivo,

I have been mulling over what to write for some time. It's difficult to put into words how truely enjoyable, hilarious and inspiring it has been to work alongside you. I am a better man and chef since knowing you. Your attitude, personality and wisdom have made QV a real pleasure for me and everyone else who you have crossed paths with.

Looking forward to plenty more spilled drinks together matey. Doug x

FROM THE EARTH

World's Great, Rare and Almost Forgotten Vegetables

PETER GILMORE

Photography by Brett Stevens

Hardie Grant

BOOKS

INTRODUCTION

I planted my first vegetable garden about twelve years ago when, for the first time in my adult life, I moved into a house with a reasonably sized backyard. I started with a herb garden and experimented with a few vegetables and was instantly hooked. The idea that you can plant a small seed – a pea seed, say – into the soil and, within a few days, a green shoot appears from the earth. This green shoot grows into a more substantial plant, climbing a trellis and bursting into flower. These flowers then attract insects for pollination. Small pea pods begin to emerge from the flowers and, as they grow, young peas develop inside the pods. It's hard to believe that planting just one seed creates so much life, beauty and sustenance. If the pods are left on the plant and allowed to mature further, the peas will eventually dry, providing new seeds, hundreds of them from a single plant, which can be saved, stored and used to grow new plants for next season. Of course, I knew this was *how* it worked, but I hadn't experienced it firsthand before. I just hadn't realised how wonderful the process was – what a truly, deeply amazing gift nature provides us.

Then I discovered just how many remarkable varieties of vegetables are actually available. I started to devour seed catalogues and my humble garden bed grew to take over the whole of the backyard including my sons' soccer pitch, which they were not impressed with! I remember buying them a trampoline to make up for it, thinking the trampoline would take up a lot less space. But it wasn't long before I was planting potatoes underneath it ...

As a chef, I also began to question why I couldn't buy some of the varieties I was growing for the restaurant. I wanted to start using purple and white carrots, not just orange ones, in my cooking. I wanted to use some of the amazing varieties of radishes that I was growing – the ones that were the colour of ripe watermelon inside – as well as the beautiful flowers of the peas I was growing. Back then I couldn't find these in the Australian marketplace, so I decided to approach the farmers directly. I met with a couple of local market farmers who grew close to Sydney and asked them, 'Would you grow multi-coloured carrots and pea flowers for me?' but was met with, 'Carrots are orange, mate' and 'No, I'm not going to grow a field of peas for you and go out each morning and pick flowers. If I grow peas, I'll plant a whole field, wait until the peas are ready, go out and pick the whole field and send them to market just the once'.

Eventually I found some like-minded, passionate, small-scale growers who were willing to work with me. They were prepared to grow more unusual, often heirloom, varieties for the restaurant and I was willing to pay a premium for them. It gave me a much wider palette of beautiful ingredients to work from and the deal gave them a new market and a better livelihood. It was the beginning of a new revolution in produce here in Australia, a direct relationship between farmer and restaurant with no middleman. Of course this type of thing had been happening in Europe for decades but it wasn't really happening in Australia back then. Most city restaurants simply placed an order with a fruit and vegetable distributor who just bought what was available at the markets. My small-scale farmers gradually became bigger and were able to start supplying other Sydney restaurants directly as well. Fast forward a decade or so and a lot of the produce that I wasn't able to buy back then is now much more readily available in the general marketplace. I feel very proud that I have played a small part in the growth of this diversity.

During this time my home garden continued to grow. I moved house seven years ago with the express purpose of finding a bigger backyard to grow more myself, which I did. I now call my home garden the 'test garden', and each season I grow as many new vegetable varieties (or, in fact, often old varieties) as I can find to see what's useful, flavourful and interesting. I also now have a great network of small-scale farmers who will grow my new discoveries for the restaurants. I love working closely with them; we have to plan what they will grow for me each season three to four months ahead, which means I also need to plan my menus months ahead. It can be a challenge and I need to commit to a certain amount of produce that needs to be succession-planted by the farmers to provide stability of supply over a season. Though there are no guarantees when it comes to nature. Heat, cold, low germination rates, pests, rainfall and many other factors all play their part and I have to be prepared to change my menu if things do not go to plan. But when it all comes together, it is quite magical.

WHY HEIRLOOM?

Biodiversity

Through observation of the natural world and selective breeding techniques, our ancestors have allowed us to accumulate a legacy of biodiversity that has enriched our lives. Sadly, today we are in danger of losing much of this diversity that has taken centuries to create. Heirloom varieties that were once popular as little as fifty years ago are disappearing from our grocery stores, food chains and even our seed catalogues. Once an heirloom vegetable ceases to be grown and the seeds are not saved for a couple of seasons, it will become extinct and the unique characteristics of that plant, which are often chance happenings of nature, will also be lost. Some heirloom varietals are often kept alive only in one small area, village or even by just one family through the generations. Certain characteristics of these heirlooms may provide the key to disease resistance or drought tolerance in the crops of the future. If all we grow is one or two commercial varieties of a certain vegetable we leave ourselves open and vulnerable to disease and crop failures. We must protect biodiversity.

Flavour

As a chef and a person who loves food, I am particularly interested in preserving the unique flavours and textures found in these heirlooms. Many older varieties have unique variations in flavour and texture. These heirloom varieties were often bred and selected with flavour being the driving factor, something that can be overlooked in modern plant breeding where efforts are often directed towards yield and durability.

Collective inheritance

Another important characteristic of heirloom vegetables is that they are open-pollinated, meaning the seeds can be saved and replanted year after year. No one owns or controls these plants; they are our collective inheritance. This is so important in our modern world of corporate ownership, patents and general control of our food systems by huge multinational companies. I'm not saying that all modern plant breeding is bad. Through natural crossbreeding techniques some F1 varietals are very useful. Small amounts of royalties for the efforts of breeding new varietals with exceptional flavour and high yields has merit, although it is important that we don't lose our open-pollinated varieties as it can become very easy for farmers to lose control of their farms and their rights if they have to rely on big companies to buy new seeds each season. F1 varieties are usually bred by the cross-pollination of two different varieties in the same plant family to create or bring to the fore certain characteristics. After all, this is nature's way of creating new varieties. With continued selection and breeding through several generations, a crossbred vegetable can become a stable new variety that can be open-pollinated and established in its own right.

Avoiding genetic modification

Genetically modified (GM) plants are a whole different matter. These plants are bred in a laboratory at a cellular level, often with genes from completely unrelated organisms. Some of these genetic crosses have no chance of occurring naturally. It is my understanding that most research and development of GM plants is being done by multinational companies for the purpose of making those crops resistant to particular types of pesticides – for example, inserting genes from organisms such as bacteria into corn and wheat with the aim of making those plants resistant to the pesticides that are sprayed on them; the pesticides kill the weeds but do not kill the crop. I know for sure that I don't want to consume that wheat or corn. It seems to me that this kind of manipulation of our plants is more about the control and ownership of our food systems by large pesticide companies. This seems crazy when so much valuable research and development can come from more natural plant-breeding techniques. I believe that GM food has not been given the research and time it needs to be considered safe. This affects all of us – our health and our rights as human beings – especially in Australia, where our own government refuses to label food containing GM material. This takes away our rights to have the knowledge and choice about the food we eat and, once GM crops are out there in our fields, it's almost impossible to control cross-contamination. While this book is not about the politics of food, it is important to be aware of these issues and I urge you to read up on it further elsewhere. This book is about embracing the beauty of our vegetable diversity, exploring it, treasuring it and realising the need to protect it.

ABOUT THIS BOOK

From the Earth is a celebration of the incredible diversity that can be found in the world of vegetables. It is about how nature and humans have worked together throughout the centuries to produce an extraordinary range of edible plants that sustain us.

In this book I am looking at mostly heirloom and open-pollinated varieties of vegetables and fruiting vegetables. There are so many varieties I could have included – literally hundreds. I have settled on the vegetables I have grown myself that have excited me over the years for their culinary potential. Some are more common varietals of heirlooms that are special to me. Some are rare, some are almost extinct. Some have only recently been reintroduced to seed companies through the efforts of just one family. Some have been introduced to the wider world from one small area or a remote valley that has grown a particular vegetable for generations. Some of the seeds have been found by archaeologists in a ball of ancient clay that has preserved the seeds. It has been twelve years now since I first started growing vegetables and I have searched seed companies all over Australia and the world for some of the seeds I have grown during that time. It has become a passion of mine to protect and save these seeds as well – one that has also informed and inspired my work as a chef.

In this book, as well as talking a little about the history and provenance of some of my favourite vegetables, I have included a recipe for every one that I feature. Some recipes are from my Sydney restaurants Quay and Bennelong, while others are from my home kitchen. Some are very involved, while others are very simple. Some are vegetarian, some are not, but all are about bringing out the best in these special vegetables. I hope you enjoy this book and that it inspires you to embrace the diversity of the vegetable world yourself.

A note on availability

I am aware that it may be difficult to find a lot of the varieties and cultivars I talk about in this book unless you grow them yourself, and to cook some of the recipes you may need to substitute in different varieties. For example, if you wish to make the tortellini on page 162 you could substitute the Melonette Jaspee for a butternut squash. In some cases making substitutions will be harder and the results will have a different flavour profile, but I urge you to use the recipes as a starting point to experiment with all sorts of varieties.

A note on measurements

This book uses metric cup measurements, i.e. 250 ml (8½ fl oz) for 1 cup; in the US a cup is 237 ml (8 fl oz), so American cooks should be generous with their cup measurements; in the UK, a cup is 284 ml (9½ fl oz), so British cooks should be scant with their cup measurements. Similarly, 20 ml (¾ fl oz) tablespoons are used; cooks with 15 ml (½ fl oz) tablespoons should be generous with their tablespoon measurements.

Country Gentleman Corn

FAMILY
POACEAE

SPECIES
ZEA MAYS

CULTIVAR
COUNTRY GENTLEMAN

Country Gentleman is an heirloom corn variety developed and introduced to the American market in 1890 by S.D. Woodruff & Sons. It has milky white kernels that are tightly and unevenly packed in zigzag-like patterns referred to as 'shoepegs', which I love. When picked young, this corn is deliciously sweet. —— Also referred to as zea-mays or maize, corn belongs to the *Poaceae* family of flowering plants known as grasses, which includes many cereal crops such as maize, wheat, rice, barley, oats and millet (other relatives in this family group include lemongrass, rye, sugarcane and bamboo). Archaeological evidence shows that corn has been cultivated for some 7000 years – its genetic lineage can be traced back to Central America and Mexico from a selection of wild grasses called teosintes and it is thought that naturally occurring mutations, together with human selection of certain species, transformed these into the cultivated plant we know today. —— When growing corn, it is important to remember to plant it in groups or blocks rather than single rows; being wind-pollinated, this will aid better pollination. Corn prefers full sun and needs a nutrient-rich, loamy soil to grow well. In cooler climates corn seeds should be planted once the soil is beginning to warm and there is no danger of frosts. From seed to harvest will be about 90 days. —— Corn is a majestic plant to watch grow from the initial shoot to its towering 2.4 m (8 ft) height. Watching its tassels sway in the wind and knowing that pollination is underway gives me a sense of anticipation for the ripening cobs beginning to form. The joy of picking a ripe cob in the height of summer and peeling back its husk to expose the milky white jewels makes the wait worthwhile.

SOFT WHITE POLENTA, COUNTRY GENTLEMAN CORN

When picked young at what you call the 'milk' stage, Country Gentleman corn is one of the sweetest white heritage corns available. This dish is a celebration of corn – a soft white corn polenta is served with blanched Country Gentleman kernels heated in a sauce made from white corn juice and finished with a white corn emulsion. This dish is also excellent served with some freshly picked spanner crab meat.

NOTE: *The white corn emulsion calls for a whipping syphon (cream whipper), as well as a cold-press juicer. You could use a standard juicer at a push, but a cold-press juicer will produce far superior results.*

WHITE POLENTA

40 g (1½ oz) unsalted butter
1 shallot, finely diced
1 garlic clove, finely diced
1.2 litres (41 fl oz) Chicken Stock or Vegetable Stock
    (see Basics, page 240)
200 g (7 oz/1⅓ cups) fine white corn polenta
60 g (2 oz) parmesan, finely grated

Melt half the butter in a heavy-based saucepan, add the shallot and garlic and gently sauté until translucent. Warm the chicken or vegetable stock in a separate saucepan.

Add the polenta to the garlic and shallot mixture and stir together well, then add a ladleful of the hot stock. Continue to cook over a low heat, stirring, until the stock has been absorbed, then keep adding ladlefuls of stock, stirring with a whisk to break up any lumps and allowing each ladleful to be absorbed before adding the next, until all the stock has been absorbed (this will take about 20 minutes in total). Cook for a further 10 minutes, stirring regularly, then remove from the heat and whisk in the parmesan and remaining butter. Set aside to cool completely. (For a superfine mouth-feel, press the polenta through a fine-mesh drum sieve before cooling.)

WHITE CORN EMULSION

4 young Country Gentleman corn cobs, kernels removed
4 egg yolks
½ teaspoon lemon juice
1 teaspoon water
250 ml (8½ fl oz/1 cup) melted butter
sea salt

Pass the corn kernels through a cold-press juicer. Measure out 400 ml (13½ fl oz) of the corn juice, setting aside 200 ml (7 fl oz) for later use.

Put the egg yolks in a stainless-steel bowl. Bring a saucepan of water, large enough for the bowl to fit on top of, to a gentle simmer. Add the lemon juice, water and 200 ml (7 fl oz) of the corn juice to the eggs and whisk well, then place the bowl on top of the saucepan and whisk the mixture until it's thick enough to coat the back of a spoon. Gradually add the melted butter, whisking as you go, and cook for 3–4 minutes until you have a thick hollandaise-like sauce. Season to taste with salt, then transfer the emulsion to a charged whipping syphon (cream whipper) and set aside in a warm part of the kitchen.

Additional ingredients

80 g (2¾ oz) crème fraîche
zest and juice of ½ lemon
sea salt
200 ml (7 fl oz) reserved white corn juice (as left)
20 g (¾ oz) unsalted butter
4 young Country Gentleman corn cobs, kernels removed

To serve

Reheat the polenta, whisking, over a low heat. Stir in the crème fraîche, lemon zest and juice and season with sea salt to taste. Keep warm.

Whisk together the white corn juice and butter in a saucepan set over a medium heat for about 2 minutes, or until the corn juice naturally thickens. Blanch the corn kernels in a separate saucepan of boiling salted water for 1 minute, then drain and add them to the thickened corn juice. Season with sea salt to taste.

Place a generous spoonful of polenta in the centre of each warmed serving plate, top with the white corn kernels and juice and finish with the white corn emulsion from the syphon. Serve.

Kyoto Red Carrot

FAMILY

APIACEAE (UMBELLIFERAE)

SPECIES

DAUCUS CAROTA SUBSP. *SATIVUS*

CULTIVAR

KYOTO RED

This Japanese *kintoki* (sweet red) carrot is considered one of the *dento yasai* (traditional or heirloom) vegetables of the Kyoto region and is famed for its deep red colour, sweetness and tender texture. It is often carved into the shape of a plum blossom to represent fertility for Japanese New Year. —— Derived from the wild plant Queen Anne's Lace, with its large lacy flowers and long yellow taproot, carrots belong to the *Apiaceae* family and count parsnips, celery, fennel, caraway, dill and parsley among their relatives. Originally purple and yellow, cultivated carrots are believed to have originated in the region of Afghanistan around the 10th century. From here they diverged, spreading both east and west; Western carrot cultivation spread to Spain in the 12th century via the Middle East and North Africa (there are many accounts of white and orange carrots being grown in Western Europe in texts from the 17th century), while red carrots appeared in China and Japan around the early 17th century. —— The famous heirloom Kyoto Red carrot is mainly grown through autumn and into winter. The deep red colour – derived from the antioxidant lycopene, which is considered to have many health benefits – becomes prominent when the carrots are at full maturity and the ground is cold. I love the striking appearance of these carrots and I often cook them slowly (they do not tend to break up during cooking) to bring out their tenderness and sweetness.

KYOTO RED CARROT SALAD WITH
SHEEP'S MILK FETA, SMOKED ALMONDS, SHERRY CARAMEL

SERVES 8

I developed this deceptively simple dish for the Cured & Cultured bar at Bennelong restaurant, where it has remained on the menu since the opening. The combination of flavours and textures in this salad is simply delicious. We intensify the flavour of the carrots by first cooking them in carrot juice and then slow roasting, while the contrast of the salty, creamy feta, crunchy smoked almonds and sherry caramel take things way beyond expectations.

NOTE: *This recipe makes more sherry caramel than you need, but it stores well in the refrigerator; use it to dress a range of salads or drizzle it over sliced ripe tomatoes.*

SLOW-COOKED CARROTS

8 medium-sized Kyoto Red carrots, peeled
1–1.5 litres (34–51 fl oz/4–6 cups) fresh carrot juice
extra-virgin olive oil
sea salt
caster (superfine) sugar

Place the carrots in a vacuum-seal bag with 1 litre (34 fl oz/4 cups) of the carrot juice. Seal the bag, removing all the air, and cook in a steamer at 90°C (195°F) for 15 minutes, then leave the carrots to cool in the bag. Alternatively, bring 1.5 litres (51 fl oz/6 cups) carrot juice to a simmer in a saucepan, add the carrots and blanch for 10 minutes, then leave to cool in the liquid.

Preheat the oven to 200°C (400°F). Place the carrots on a wire rack, drizzle with a little olive oil and sprinkle over a little salt and sugar, then transfer to the oven and roast for 10 minutes. Remove and leave to cool to room temperature, then chop into 2 cm (¾ in) chunks on the diagonal. Set aside until needed.

SHERRY CARAMEL

375 ml (12½ fl oz/1½ cups) oloroso sherry
150 g (5½ oz/⅔ cup) caster (superfine) sugar
150 ml (5 fl oz) sherry vinegar

Combine 300 ml (10 fl oz) of the sherry with the sugar in a heavy-based saucepan and stir to dissolve. Heat until the mixture reaches 160°C (320°F) or a light caramel forms. Add the remaining 75 ml (2½ fl oz) sherry – being careful, as hot caramel will spit – then remove from the heat and stir well. Leave to cool to room temperature, then whisk in the sherry vinegar, transfer to an airtight container and set aside in the refrigerator until needed.

CARROT PURÉE

75 g (2¾ oz) unsalted butter
60 g (2 oz) shallots, finely diced
300 g (10½ oz) carrots, chopped
300 ml (10 fl oz) fresh carrot juice
water
sea salt and freshly ground black pepper

Melt the butter in a heavy-based saucepan, add the shallots and sauté over a medium heat until translucent. Add the carrots and carrot juice, top up with a small amount of water to ensure the carrots are just covered and simmer over a high heat until the carrots are soft and most of the juice has evaporated. Place in a food processor or blender and blend on high speed for 1 minute, then pass the purée through a fine-mesh sieve. Season to taste and leave to chill in the refrigerator until needed.

Additional ingredients

2 tablespoons extra-virgin olive oil
120 g (4½ oz) sheep's milk feta
2 baby orange carrots, finely sliced
100 g (3½ oz) smoked and toasted almonds
30 g (1 oz) puffed amaranth
about 30 linaria flowers (optional) or other edible flowers

To serve

Add the slow-cooked carrot chunks and olive oil to a large bowl and mix together well. Place the oiled carrot chunks in the middle of a large serving platter, crumble over the feta and scatter over the sliced baby carrots and smoked almonds. Dot teaspoons of the carrot purée over the salad in a random pattern and drizzle over 2 tablespoons of the sherry caramel. Garnish with puffed amaranth and linaria flowers, if you like. Serve.

Black Chickpea

FAMILY

FABACEAE

SPECIES

CICER ARIETINUM

CULTIVAR

CECI NERI DELLA MURGIA

With an estimated ten million hectares across the world dedicated to growing them, chickpeas are one of the most important pulse crops on earth. A legume of the *Fabaceae* family, the chickpea is believed to have originated in the fertile crescent of modern Turkey, Syria and Iran. It is one of the earliest cultivated legumes, with chickpea remains found in the Middle East dating back to around 7000 BC. Having been gradually introduced to the Mediterranean region, chickpeas reached the Indian subcontinent by 2000 BC. —— Chickpeas are cheap to buy – much cheaper than most protein sources – and contain a wide range of amino acids. High in fibre, low in fat and containing phosphorous, calcium and iron, they are widely used in Middle Eastern dishes such as falafel and hummus as well as stews and soups. On the Indian subcontinent they form an important part of a predominantly vegetarian diet, where they are also processed into a flour (besan) used to cook bhaji, pakoras, breads and some dhals. —— There are many cultivars of chickpeas, but they generally fall into two main groups: desi (microsperma) cultivars, which produce smaller, darker seeds and are predominantly found in the Indian subcontinent, Ethiopia and Iran; and kabuli (macrosperma) cultivars, which produce relatively large, plump seeds with a smooth, cream-coloured coat and are largely grown through Afghanistan, North Africa, western Asia, southern Europe and the West. —— Chickpeas thrive in a sunny site with a cool, dry climate and a well-drained soil (they are generally grown on heavy black or red soils with a pH of 5.5–8.6). While chickpeas can be cultivated in tropical and subtropical climates, they do not do well in humid and low-lying tropical areas with excessive rains. —— The Ceci Neri della Murgia chickpea is a desi cultivar, though larger in size and with an even darker black colour than the ones found in India. It was grown in the southern regions of Murgia in Apulia during the 19th century as an important protein source for rural families – though, over time, it almost disappeared from cultivation, falling out of production for more profitable crops such as olives and grapes. Being listed by the Slow Food Foundation has helped revive these black chickpeas, bringing them to the attention of artisan food importers and chefs, with six farmers from a local Slow Food Presidium having started to produce them again using integrated farming techniques. —— The pods of Ceci Neri della Murgia can be harvested while they are still green; each contains two small chickpeas that are initially green in colour with a tinge of black – it is only once fully dried that the seeds become jet black in colour. (There are other chickpea cultivars that remain green even after they are dried and there exists a red variety of chickpea that, despite my best efforts, I have not yet been able to track down.) I love these particular chickpeas for their nutty, rich flavour and striking black colour, and find them easy to grow in my home garden in Sydney.

BLACK CHICKPEAS SLOWLY BRAISED IN ROASTED ONION JUICE

SERVES 8

The striking black chickpeas are the star of this dish. Their flavour is enhanced by cooking them slowly in a roasted onion juice, adding a depth and complexity that is set off by a little garlic cream and some fried wakame seaweed.

NOTE: *This recipe calls for a cold-press juicer. A cold-press juicer will produce far superior results in terms of flavour and texture, but you can use a standard juicer at a push.*

CHICKPEAS

400 g (14 oz) black chickpeas
1.5 litres (51 fl oz/6 cups) filtered water

Add the chickpeas to a bowl, cover with the water and leave to soak overnight.

ROASTED ONION JUICE

1 kg (2 lb 3 oz) rock salt
10 large brown onions
100 g (3½ oz) shiitake mushrooms, sliced
1 x 10 cm (4 in) square dried kombu seaweed
1 tablespoon brown-rice vinegar

Preheat the oven to 200°C (400°F) and cover a baking tray in a layer of rock salt. Cut each onion in half, leaving the skins intact, then place the onion halves, cut side up, on the rock salt. Roast for 45 minutes, or until the onions are well coloured and soft to the touch. Dust the salt off the onion halves, then transfer to a large bowl, cover with plastic wrap and leave for 30 minutes to sweat.

Once sweated, strain and reserve the onion juice and pass the onion flesh through a cold-press juicer. Strain and combine the extracted juice with the reserved onion juice in a heavy-based saucepan, then bring to a gentle boil together with the sliced shiitake mushrooms and cook until reduced by half. Remove from the heat and add the kombu seaweed and vinegar. Leave to cool, then strain, discarding the solids. Set aside.

GARLIC CREAM

24 garlic cloves, peeled
1.5 litres (51 fl oz/6 cups) milk
50 g (1¾ oz) unsalted butter
2 shallots, finely diced
20 g (¾ oz) inner celery stalk, white part only, finely diced
500 ml (17 fl oz/2 cups) Vegetable Stock (see Basics, page 240)
2 tablespoons crème fraîche
sea salt

Add the garlic cloves and 500 ml (17 fl oz/2 cups) of the milk to a saucepan. Bring to a simmer and cook for 2 minutes, then strain the garlic and discard the milk. Return the garlic to the pan and repeat this process twice more. (Triple blanching your garlic like this helps to reduce the intensity of its flavour, preventing it from being overpowering in the finished cream.) Melt the butter in a separate saucepan, add the shallot and celery and gently sauté until translucent. Add the blanched garlic and vegetable stock and simmer until virtually all the liquid has evaporated, then transfer the mixture to a food processor or blender and blitz on high speed for 1 minute until smooth. Pass through a fine-mesh sieve, stir in the crème fraîche and season with sea salt. Refrigerate until needed.

Additional ingredients (optional)

2 tablespoons shredded dried wakame, soaked in cold water for 1–2 hours and patted dry
500 ml (17 fl oz/2 cups) grapeseed oil
sea salt

To serve

If garnishing with seaweed, place the wakame on a baking tray and semi-dehydrate in a dehydrator or a very low oven preheated to 80°C (175°F) for 2 hours, or until the seaweed is quite dry but still flexible. Heat the grapeseed oil to 180°C (350°F) in a large saucepan, add the semi-dehydrated seaweed in small batches and fry until crispy. Drain on paper towel and set aside in an airtight container until needed.

Drain the soaked chickpeas, place them in a medium saucepan and pour over enough cold water to cover them by 10 cm (4 in). Bring to a gentle boil and cook for 15–20 minutes, adding additional water if necessary, until tender. Strain the chickpeas and transfer them to a clean saucepan with the reduced onion juice. Bring to a simmer over a medium–high heat and cook for a further 20 minutes, or until the chickpeas have absorbed most but not all of the onion juice. Season with sea salt to taste.

Reheat the garlic cream. Place a large spoonful of chickpeas in the centre of each bowl and ladle over some of the excess juice. Top with a spoonful of garlic cream and garnish with the fried seaweed, if using.

Gete Okosomin Squash

FAMILY
CUCURBITACEAE

SPECIES
CUCURBITA MAXIMA

CULTIVAR
GETE OKOSOMIN

Gete Okosomin, which translates literally as 'big old squash', is a wonderful pre-Columbian variety of squash originally grown by native Americans in the area now known as Wisconsin. Believed to be extinct until recent times, the squash gained fame online when it became known as the '800-year-old squash' whose seed was found in a clay ball on an archaeological dig in 2008 on Menominee nation land in Wisconsin. —— Although this story is very romantic (and native American peoples did indeed store their seeds in clay pots that were designed to protect them from rodents and insects), according to Kenton Lobe, an environmental studies professor at Canada's Mennonite University in Winnipeg, the truth is a little less theatrical, though no less captivating. He believes that the seeds came from elderly gardeners of the native American Miami people in Indiana, who gifted them to David Wrone, a professor at the university of Wisconsin, in 1995. Wrone said the seeds had not laid dormant for centuries but that the Miami people had been growing them for as long as 5000 years, taking care to hand-pollinate them to maintain their purity over time. Wrone then grew the squash and shared the second generation of seeds with his neighbours, including some with the Menominee nation. Over time, the seeds travelled across the Midwest (and every time the seeds changed hands, the legend of their origins grew a little more exciting) before they finally turned up at the American Indian centre of Chicago and the White Earth seed library. —— Whatever the truth behind its origins, the Gete Okosomin squash reveals the rich agricultural knowledge and history of the native American peoples. I first heard about this squash from Baker Creek Heirloom Seeds, and grew it for the first time last year. It is certainly an impressive vegetable. The colour is a rich, bright orange with lighter orange stripes running down its length. The squash I grew was close to 1 m (3 ft) long, an impressive sight to see among the vines, and its flesh was delicious and sweet with a smooth, rich texture.

FETTUCINE OF GETE OKOSOMIN SQUASH, BROWN BUTTER, FENNEL POLLEN

SERVES 8

Possessing a nutty intensity when roasted, but an equally fine, crisp flavour when barely blanched, the Gete Okosomin squash lends itself to a variety of preparations. In this dish I have combined these two cooking techniques, with the end result enhanced through the use of brown butter, bronze fennel and fennel pollen.

24 fennel flowers
1 kg (2 lb 3 oz) rock salt
200 ml (7 fl oz) Brown Butter (see Basics, page 241), melted
1 Gete Okosomin squash (approx. 700 g/1 lb 9 oz)
sea salt
1 bunch bronze fennel fronds, separated

Using your fingers, crumble 16 of the fennel flowers over a dish to collect the pollen. Discard the flower stalks and set aside the pollen until needed.

Preheat the oven to 180°C (350°F) and cover a baking tray in a layer of rock salt. Melt the brown butter in a small saucepan.

Cut the Gete Okosomin squash in half lengthways and remove the seeds. Place one half, cut side up, on the rock salt, brush with 50 ml (1¾ fl oz) of the brown butter and sprinkle with sea salt. Roast for approximately 90 minutes, or until lightly golden brown and well softened.

Meanwhile, cut the remaining squash half into quarters and peel away the skin, then cut each piece into 2 mm (⅛ in) thick strips using a mandoline or sharp knife. Cut the strips lengthways into 1 cm (½ in) thick ribbons, keeping them as long as possible so they resemble fettucine.

Bring a large pot of salted water to the boil.

Remove the roasted squash from the oven. Using a tablespoon, scoop sections of the roasted squash flesh from the skin and transfer them to warmed serving plates. Press lightly down on each piece of squash with the back of the spoon, drizzle over a little brown butter and season with sea salt.

Briefly blanch the squash ribbons in the boiling water for a maximum of 30 seconds, then drain and toss in the remaining brown butter, seasoning with sea salt and sprinkling over the fennel pollen to finish. Place a generous bundle of the squash fettucine on top of each piece of roasted squash and garnish with the fennel fronds and remaining fennel flowers. Serve.

Mitoyo Eggplant

FAMILY
SOLANACEAE

SPECIES
SOLANUM MELONGENA

CULTIVAR
MITOYO

The eggplant, or aubergine, is a species of domesticated nightshade related to the tomato and potato. It has a long history of cultivation – appearing in Sanskrit and Chinese agro-botanical literature dating back 2000 years – though its lack of Ancient Greek or Roman names, together with the numerous Arabic and northern African names that exist for it, indicate it was introduced throughout the Mediterranean region by the Arabs in the early Middle Ages. (The eggplant is unrecorded in England until the 16th century.) —— Although the origins of the eggplant's domestication are unclear – with botanists divided over whether its roots lie in Southeast or Central Asia – we do know that the cultivars we are familiar with today were gradually improved over hundreds of years of man's intervention; selecting seeds to grow in the next season only from plants with preferred qualities (better flavour, bigger fruit, smoother stems etc.). The Mitoyo eggplants, traditionally grown in the Mitoyo and Kanonji areas of Japan, are small- to medium-sized teardrop-shaped eggplants with a nearly black skin and matching dark stem. The flesh is extremely tender and sweet, so much so that it can be consumed raw, although traditionally these eggplants are roasted or grilled and also make excellent pickles. —— A warm-season crop needing temperatures between 21–30°C (70–86°F) to do well, eggplant grows year-round in the tropics and most of the year in the subtropics, though in cooler temperature zones seedlings may need to be started indoors before being grown out in the summer months. It performs best in a rich, free-draining soil, preferring slightly acidic conditions with a pH of 5.5. To avoid a possible build-up of pests and disease, it is best not planted in beds where other nightshade family members have recently been grown. When I grew the Mitoyo eggplant in my home garden I found the plant to be extremely vigorous, being the first of the six varieties I grew that season to flower and fruit, and with a single plant producing at least a dozen delicious eggplants.

ROASTED MITOYO EGGPLANT,
XO, STREAKY BACON

This is a cheeky, spicy dish that relies on the warmth and strength of the XO sauce and my fondness for crispy bacon to highlight the creamy, unctuous texture of these little Japanese eggplants.

220 ml (7½ fl oz) grapeseed oil
1½ teaspoons finely diced garlic
1½ teaspoons finely diced fresh ginger
1 tablespoon finely diced shallot
1½ teaspoons finely diced dried scallop
1½ teaspoons finely diced dried shiitake mushroom
2 tablespoons gochujang (Korean fermented red chilli paste)
500 ml (17 fl oz/2 cups) Chicken Stock (see Basics, page 240)
juice of ¼ lemon
8 small Mitoyo eggplants (aubergines)
16 thinly sliced streaky bacon rashers (slices)

For the XO sauce, heat 20 ml (¾ fl oz) of the grapeseed oil in a heavy-based saucepan over a medium heat, add the garlic, ginger and shallot and sauté until translucent. Add the diced scallop and shiitake mushroom and sauté for a further minute, then stir in the gochujang, pour over the chicken stock and mix together well. Bring to a vigorous simmer and reduce down for 15–20 minutes, or until you are left with about 150 ml (5 fl oz) of liquid. Remove the sauce from the heat and set aside until needed (it will keep in the refrigerator for up to 1 week).

Mix 100 ml (3½ fl oz) of the grapeseed oil together with the lemon juice. Cut the eggplants in half lengthways and brush them all over with the lemon juice and grapeseed oil mixture, then place the eggplant halves into a vacuum-seal bag and seal, removing all the air. Steam the eggplants on high for 25 minutes (alternatively, you can steam them directly in a steamer if you do not have a vacuum-seal bag). Set aside to cool to room temperature.

Preheat the oven to 180°C (350°F). Fry off the bacon in a non-stick frying pan until crispy, drain on paper towel and leave to cool, then break into large pieces. Set aside.

Heat the remaining grapeseed oil in a heavy-based ovenproof frying pan over a high heat. Add the eggplant halves to the pan, cut side down, and fry for 1½–2 minutes until well coloured. Turn the eggplant halves over, transfer the pan to the oven and cook for a further 3–4 minutes, until dark golden.

Meanwhile, warm the XO sauce in a small saucepan, add the crispy bacon pieces and stir to coat well.

Remove the eggplant halves from the oven and drain on paper towel, then divide among individual warmed serving bowls. Top with the XO-coated crispy bacon and serve immediately.

Elephant Garlic Scapes

FAMILY
AMARYLLIDACEAE

SPECIES
ALLIUM AMPELOPRASUM

CULTIVAR
ELEPHANT GARLIC

Producing very large, mildly flavoured cloves, Elephant garlic is a member of the larger *Alliaceae* family, which (together with garlic) includes onions and spring onions as well as leeks. The plants contained within this family have been cultivated for millennia; garlic in particular has been mentioned as part of the diet on Sumerian cuneiform tablets dating back to 2300 BC, as well as being used as funeral offerings in Ancient Egypt, while references to it appear in both the Bible and the Koran. —— Elephant garlic itself was 'rediscovered' in 1941 by the American nurseryman Jim Nicholls, who found it growing wild in the Willamette valley of Oregon in the gardens of Scio – an abandoned settlement originally colonised in 1860 by immigrants from the Eastern Balkans. Nicholls collected a few kilos of the giant garlic (referred to locally as Scio's giant garlic) and selectively bred it over a period of twelve years, establishing a very hardy disease-free strain that he started selling commercially in 1953 under the registered name 'Elephant Garlic'. —— There is some conjecture over the botanical status of Elephant garlic, though while botanists might still be arguing over the correct name, it is clearly a distinct type. Despite being classified by Professor James R Bagget of the University of Oregon as *Allium scorodoprasum*, British botanist Martyn Rix regards it as a form of *Allium ampeloprasum* – the wild garlic from which the leek *(Allium porrum)* was derived – a native of the eastern Mediterranean known as 'great-headed garlic' once grown in 17th century England by the famous botanist and gardener John Tradescant the Younger. Rix has no doubt that this is the cultivar rediscovered by Nicholls in Oregon. —— Like most garlic, Elephant garlic is generally planted in mid-autumn, with the mature garlic harvested in summer. It requires a nutrient-rich, well-drained soil and benefits from an addition of well-rotted manure compost in spring. In the same manner as all hard-neck garlics, Elephant garlic produces a flowering spike, known as a scape, which emerges from the leaves generally in late spring. While most garlic growers remove and discard these scapes so that the plant can direct all its energy into growing the bulbs, these tender green stems are – when carefully peeled, sliced and sautéed – delicious. With fatter, juicier stems (especially towards the base) and a generally sweeter, milder flavour than regular garlic, I have found Elephant garlic scapes to be particularly good.

SPRING LAMB WITH ELEPHANT GARLIC SCAPES

SERVES 8

With their succulent texture and gentle garlic flavour, garlic scapes are a seasonal treat that partners beautifully with spring lamb. Here, their subtle sweetness is contrasted with the intensity of a small amount of fermented black garlic paste.

1 x Black Garlic Paste (see page 210)
8 x 4-rib lamb racks
sea salt
2 tablespoons extra-virgin olive oil
100 g (3½ oz) unsalted butter
16 Elephant garlic scapes, peeled and finely sliced
about 30 golden orach sprigs or young spinach sprouts
about 40 broad (fava) bean flowers or other
edible flowers

Preheat the oven to 180°C (350°F). Warm the black garlic paste in a small saucepan.

Place one of the lamb racks on a chopping board. Using a sharp knife, carefully cut around the loin and remove it from the bone. Trim off any sinew, then repeat with the remaining lamb racks. Season the lamb loins well with sea salt.

Heat the oil in a large frying pan set over a high heat. Working in batches, add the lamb loins and seal on all sides. Arrange the sealed loins on a wire rack, transfer to the oven and roast for approximately 4–5 minutes, or until medium-rare. Remove from the oven and set aside to rest.

Melt the butter in a frying pan, add the scapes and sauté over a medium heat for 1 minute, until wilted but still vibrant and green. Remove from the heat and season with sea salt to taste.

Divide the lamb loins among serving plates and spoon over the garlic scapes. Add four or five dots of black garlic paste on top of each loin and garnish with the golden orach sprigs and broad bean flowers. Serve.

Puntarelle Chicory

FAMILY
ASTERACEAE

SPECIES
CICHORIUM INTYBUS L.

CULTIVAR
CATALOGNA PUNTARELLE DI GALATINA

Puntarelle is a most remarkable type of leaf chicory, sometimes referred to as asparagus chicory because of the swollen, asparagus-like stems that sprout from the centre of the plant as it starts to reach maturity. The shoots are unique, with a mild, attractive bitterness and a crisp texture. —— Chicories in general are thought to be a native of Eurasia, but it is the Italians who have been responsible for cultivating many of the unique forms we have today – chicory Catalogna Puntarelle di Galatina gets its name from the southern Italian town of Galatina in Puglia, where it is believed to have been first grown. —— In Italy, a chicory salad is often served between courses (traditionally, chicory has been considered a great aid for digestion and is said to stimulate the appetite) and puntarelle in particular features in the Roman salad of the same name, in which the stems are soaked in a couple of changes of cold water to help leach some of the bitterness, then thinly sliced and served with a dressing of anchovy, garlic and wine vinegar pounded and emulsified with extra-virgin olive oil. Puntarelle can also be briefly blanched in boiling water, the cooking reducing its bitterness, then dressed with olive oil and salt. I grew puntarelle last year in my home garden and soon realised each plant needed a fair bit of space around it, at least 60–70 cm (24–28 in), as they are quite vigorous. As the puntarelle initially looked similar to other chicories I had grown, I didn't think I was going to see the characteristic swollen stems develop. It turned out, however, that these form once the plant is quite mature, at which point it truly is an impressive thing to behold.

FRIED PUNTARELLE CHICORY

SERVES 8

The puntarelle chicory is quite unique in the chicory family. Famed for its swollen stems, it has the characteristic bitter flavour associated with chicories but, when cooked, that flavour becomes milder. This is a very simple recipe that uses potato flour to coat the chicory stems. You could serve these with aïoli or a yoghurt-based dipping sauce.

1 whole puntarelle chicory (endive)
2 litres (68 fl oz/8 cups) sunflower oil
250 g (9 oz/1⅔ cups) potato flour
sea salt and freshly ground black pepper
approx. 250 ml (8½ fl oz/1 cup) soda water (club soda)

Trim off the puntarelle base and remove the bitter top leaves. Cut the puntarelle stems into finger-sized pieces.

Heat the oil to 180°C (350°F) in a large saucepan.

Place the flour into a large mixing bowl, season with sea salt and pepper and whisk in enough soda water to form a thin batter. Dip the puntarelle stems into the batter, then lower into the oil and fry in small batches for 1–2 minutes until lightly golden. Season with sea salt and serve immediately.

Japanese White Turnip

FAMILY
BRASSICACEAE

SPECIES
BRASSICA RAPA VAR. RAPIFERA

CULTIVAR
TENNOUJI KABURA

White turnips are a specialty of Japan. In comparison to the robustly flavoured, yellow-fleshed and green- or purple-shouldered turnips found in the West, these Japanese turnips are so sweet and delicate that they can be eaten raw – though a light steaming only serves to increase their sweetness and tenderness. ——The turnip (or 'kabu' in Japanese) is one of the oldest vegetables to be cultivated and is said to have made its way to Japan via China and Afghanistan – a journey that must have taken place around the 8th or 9th century, as references can be found to them in ancient Japanese chronicles from this time. In the centuries that followed, more than 80 varieties of kabu evolved with varying colours, shapes and tastes, with most of these, including the red-skinned varieties that were grown in mountainous regions, being developed in isolation. This level of diversity is not seen in any other country and is what has elevated the kabu to be regarded as an iconic vegetable in Japan alongside the daikon (Japanese radish), also of the *Brassicaceae* family. —— White turnips are one of the easiest vegetables to grow. Planting in early spring can produce golf ball–sized sweet white turnips (complete with edible, delicious greens) within a six-week period, while planting in mid-autumn will produce a crop just before winter. Turnips are quite cold hardy and will resist light frosts, however they don't like the heat of summer and tend to bolt and go to seed very quickly in hot weather. —— The Tennouji Kabura turnip was originally an Osaka Tennoji district specialty. One of the oldest traditional Japanese white turnips, they thrived during the Edo era in the 18th century (during which time they were referred to by name in haiku written by Yosa Buson). These turnips are appreciated for their aroma and flavour and were traditionally used to make the *nozawana-zuke* pickles from the Nagano prefecture. Tennouji Kabura can be hard to source outside of Japan; the cultivar Tokyo Market is similar and is more widely available in the West.

STEAMED TENNOUJI KABURA TURNIP, MISO BUTTER, CHICKEN SKIN CRACKLING

SERVES 8

I love the simplicity of this dish, which belies its complexity of flavour – the Tennouji Kabura turnip is the star, with the other ingredients there to highlight and accentuate its purity and delicate sweetness.

150 g (5½ oz) chicken skin
375 ml (12½ fl oz/1½ cups) Chicken Stock (see Basics, page 240)
65 g (2¼ oz) tapioca pearls
sea salt
500 ml (17 fl oz/2 cups) sunflower oil
8 golf ball–sized Tennouji Kabura turnips (or other Japanese white turnips)
2 tablespoons melted unsalted butter
2 tablespoons yellow miso paste
1 tablespoon softened unsalted butter
zest of ½ lemon
1 teaspoon freeze-dried anchovy-based fish sauce (optional)

Scrape away and discard any fat from the chicken skin and roughly chop with a knife. Set aside.

Bring 300 ml (10 fl oz) of the chicken stock to the boil in a medium saucepan. Add the tapioca pearls, reduce the heat to a simmer and cook for 8–10 minutes, stirring every couple of minutes, until the pearls are soft and translucent. Transfer the tapioca mixture together with the chicken skin to a blender and blitz on high speed to combine, then slowly drizzle in the remaining stock, add a good pinch of salt and process for 4–5 minutes until smooth.

Spread 1 tablespoon of the mixture out between two sheets of baking paper, then use a rolling pin to help spread the mixture out evenly to a 1 mm (¹/₁₆-in) thickness. Repeat this process until you've used all the mixture, then transfer the sheets to a dehydrator or a low oven preheated to 70°C (160°F) and dehydrate for about 4 hours, or until the mixture is dried out completely.

In a large heavy-based saucepan, heat the sunflower oil to 180°C (350°F). Break the dried chicken skin sheets into small pieces approximately 4 cm (1½ in) square, then add to the pan with the hot oil in small batches and deep-fry for 30 seconds or so until puffed and golden. Drain well on paper towel and leave to cool, then store in an airtight container until needed (they will keep in the refrigerator for 2–3 days).

When ready to serve, peel the turnips and cut a 3 cm (1¼ in) thick disc from the centre of each, discarding the top and bottom, then transfer the turnip discs to a steamer placed over boiling water and steam for 2 minutes. Remove the turnips from the steamer and coat liberally with the melted butter.

Mix together the miso paste, softened butter and lemon zest in a bowl. Place a teaspoon of the mixture onto each individual warmed serving plate and top with a piece of chicken skin crackling. Divide the turnip discs among the serving plates and spoon over the fish sauce, if using (or season with a little salt if not). Serve.

Pin-striped Peanut

FAMILY
FABACEAE

SPECIES
ARACHIS HYPOGAEA

CULTIVAR
FASTIGIATA PIN-STRIPED

Although botanically classified as a legume and belonging to the *Fabaceae* (bean) family, the peanut is commonly considered and treated as a nut because it has a similar taste, texture and nutritional profile to other tree nuts. —— The cultivation of peanuts was well established in Mesoamerica long before the Spanish arrived, with archaeological evidence dating pods from a wild species to at least 7600 years ago and depictions of the nuts appearing in the art of the Moche people of ancient Peru. Later spread by European traders to tropical and subtropical locations around the world, peanuts have since become a valuable crop – used as a solid food as well as grown for their oil – with forty-two million tonnes of the shelled nuts grown in 2014 alone. —— Peanuts are an annual herbaceous plant that grow 30–50 cm (12–20 in) tall. Like most legumes, peanuts harbour symbiotic nitrogen-fixing (and soil fertility–improving) bacteria in their root nodules, making them a valuable rotation crop. The pods develop underground through an unusual reproductive feature called 'geocarpy', where the stems bend down so the pods can be embedded in the soil. Unlike peanuts bought at a store, which will have been dried thoroughly before sale, freshly harvested peanut pods initially feel softer, while the nuts themselves have a crisp, milky texture – having them at this freshest stage is only possible if you grow them yourself. —— Originating in Ecuador and covered in striking red and white stripes, the fastigiata pin-striped peanut is the first peanut plant I have grown in my home garden. The sheer diversity of nature fascinates me and, as a chef, having something as beautiful as this peanut to work with is very inspiring. It does require quite a lot of patience to grow, though; from seed I found it takes pretty much all summer for the peanuts to develop properly, and the temptation to dig underground to see how they're doing is strong! That patience is, thankfully, rewarded when you finally dig up the plants and see the fully developed peanut pods hanging from the root, not to mention when you crack open the shells and see the jewel-like nuts inside. The peanut's stripes are at their most impressive when they are used fresh – the colour remains but dulls a little when the nuts are dried and roasted.

POACHED CHICKEN, PALM HEART,
PIN-STRIPED PEANUT SALAD

The pin-striped peanut is particularly striking. Crisp, and with an almost milky flavour similar to a green almond when eaten raw and super fresh straight from the garden, it is used primarily as a textural component in this recipe.

NOTE: *The chicken poaching liquid and brown meat are not used in the finished dish here, but can be made into a soup. The ginger milk curds are at their best when just set, so should be made right before serving.*

POACHED CHICKEN

3 litres (101 fl oz/12 cups) Chicken Stock
    (see Basics, page 240)
300 ml (10 fl oz) light soy sauce
200 g (7 oz) yellow rock sugar
200 ml (7 fl oz) dry sherry
1 bunch spring onions (scallions), white part only
60 g (2 oz) fresh ginger, finely sliced
100 ml (3½ fl oz) sesame oil
1 x 1.6 kg (3½ lb) free-range chicken

Add all the ingredients except the chicken to an 8 litre (270 fl oz/32 cup) stockpot with a tight-fitting lid. Bring to the boil, reduce the heat and simmer for 15 minutes. Add the whole chicken, breast side down, to the pot, cover with the lid and return to the boil, then remove the pot from the heat and leave the chicken to poach in the hot liquid for 1 hour. Remove the chicken from the liquid and place on a draining tray, then cover with plastic wrap and transfer to the refrigerator to chill for at least 1 hour (the chicken can be poached the day before assembling the salad and chilled until needed).

EGGPLANT PURÉE

100 ml (3½ fl oz) grapeseed oil
juice of ¼ lemon
1 garlic clove, finely diced
2 eggplants (aubergines)
50 g (1¾ oz) crème fraîche
sea salt

Preheat the oven to 180°C (350°F).

Mix the grapeseed oil, lemon juice and garlic together. Slice the eggplants in half lengthways and score the flesh deeply with a sharp knife in a criss-cross pattern, leaving 1 cm (½ in) between cuts. Spread the oil, lemon juice and garlic mixture liberally over the cut flesh, wrap the eggplant halves first in baking paper and then aluminium foil to form parcels, and bake in the oven for 45 minutes. Remove from the oven and leave to cool slightly, then scoop out the flesh, leaving the skin behind.

Transfer the flesh to a food processor and blitz on high speed until smooth. Pass the purée through a fine-mesh sieve and transfer to the refrigerator until chilled. Whisk in the crème fraîche, season with sea salt and set aside until needed.

SALAD DRESSING

5 g (¼ oz/ 2 teaspoons) finely sliced fresh ginger
10 g (¼ oz/1 tablespoon) finely sliced spring onion (scallion),
    white part only
sea salt
100 ml (3½ fl oz) cold-pressed peanut oil
50 ml (1¾ fl oz) cold-pressed sesame oil

Add the ginger and spring onion to a mortar and pestle with a pinch of sea salt and grind together to form a rough paste. Gently warm the peanut and sesame oils together in a small saucepan to about 50°C (120°F), stir in the ginger and spring onion paste, remove from the heat and leave to infuse for 1 hour. Strain, discarding the solids, and set aside until required.

GINGER MILK CURDS

10 g (¼ oz/1 tablespoon) finely sliced fresh ginger
250 ml (8½ fl oz/1 cup) milk
sea salt
1 tablespoon vegetable rennet
2 teaspoons still mineral water

Add the ginger and milk to a saucepan and bring to 65°C (150°F), then remove from the heat and leave to infuse for 30 minutes. Strain and discard the solids. Season to taste with salt.

Mix the vegetable rennet and mineral water together in a separate bowl. Warm the infused milk in a small saucepan until it reaches 35°C (95°F), being careful not to allow it to overheat, then swirl the milk around in the pan to form a whirlpool. Add the vegetable rennet and water mixture to the milk, then immediately pour the contents of the saucepan into a small metal or ceramic bowl. Leave to cool and set (this should happen very quickly – you will have curds in the bowl within 1 minute).

Additional ingredients

sea salt
150 g (5½ oz) palm heart core, cut into fine strips
50 g (1¾ oz) finely sliced spring onion (scallion),
    white part only, blanched
about 60 fresh pin-striped peanuts
1 handful of kailan flower petals or other edible flower petals

To serve

Shred the chicken breast meat with your fingers and liberally dress with the prepared dressing. Season to taste with sea salt. Spread a spoonful of eggplant purée onto each serving plate, pile over the shredded chicken and garnish with the palm heart, spring onion and peanuts. Top with a spoonful of ginger milk curds and a scattering of kailan flower petals.

PALISA ANDERSON

BOON LUCK FARM

Palisa has become a good friend and one who has so impressed me with her passion for growing produce with integrity and intelligence. Her property, Boon Luck Farm, in the Byron Bay area of northern New South Wales is an inspiration to me – it supplies her family's Thai restaurants in Sydney, and I often buy her produce for Quay and Bennelong. Palisa has a very natural approach to farming (and one that I believe to be the way forward), which is kind to the earth and soil.

Palisa tells the story of how she became a farmer –

It started when we went looking for red holy basil. This Southeast Asian herb is like the holy grail in Australia for Thai cooks and the key ingredient in what seems to be our national dish, the *Padt Grapao*, a delicious herbaceous stir-fry. As luck would have it, we couldn't find a grower who could supply the amounts we needed, so we bought a farm to grow it ourselves – how naïve we were in thinking it would be as simple as that! Since then I have learnt more about our food production system than I care to know – however, that egg can't be unscrambled, and being stuck with that knowledge has led me down the rabbit hole into wanting to grow all my own food.

As city dwellers, it is too comfortable and convenient for us to buy anything we want, whenever we want it. But in pausing to consider and scrutinise the vegetable supplies we received for our restaurants, I found myself less than satisfied. The farms that supplied us weren't huge agricultural businesses, yet their practices were alarming. There were so few insects and so many perfect-looking fruit and vegetables – many that had extremely long shelf lives, and were not advisable to eat without many washes – which is just what consumers have come to expect from supermarket produce. That is what the farmers are compelled and pressured to grow to sustain their profession, often selecting varieties not for flavour but for yield and to enable them to grow their bumper-sized crops using 'conventional' methods. It is a vicious cycle, and who really – grower, retailer or consumer – benefits from this arrangement? Certainly it doesn't benefit our health or tastebuds, and it definitely doesn't benefit the soil, which is at the root of everything.

I know it's a hard sell, but I implore everyone to think again and change their mindsets when it comes to shopping for fresh produce. The tastiest and most nutritionally beneficial produce often doesn't come with long storage times before it goes off. It is often not uniform and it does often come with marks from insects … because insects know that's exactly what is good to eat! Struggling to find this produce available commercially, and with that immigrant mindset of growing our native produce in our backyards, we decided that if we wanted something we couldn't find we'd have to grow it ourselves at a scale that we could sustain.

So we ended up buying land in the Byron Bay shire. Luckily we have some wonderful resources around us up in the Northern Rivers: not only the many small organic farmers who have been generous with their experience and information, but also Elaine Ingham, a soil biologist, who has established soilfoodweb.com – an excellent educational online program teaching soil biology to the average layman like myself. Elaine's work on soil diversity at Southern Cross University, much of it based on the eroded soil of the region, greatly influenced me; her argument is that organic farming is not only about the exclusion of agricultural chemicals, or only using natural products that kill insects, weeds or diseases, but it is also about adopting a wholly integrative approach to our soil. A brief and simple summary of her argument is that we should farm in a way that allows beneficial life in the soil to build up through various methods (such as organic composting, compost teas and bioremediation), and that these additional nutrients will then help both our soil and crops better fight off undesirables like pathogens and fungal diseases. Not tilling the soil is another hugely important factor – by tilling the soil we expose it to gases that destroy our soil networks and, in turn, release more carbon dioxide (food for our crops) into the atmosphere. Instead of tilling at Boon Luck Farm we use the layering technique – whatever we grew previously gets mulched and is then immediately available for the next crop to be sown into without being ploughed in. Following this approach means we end up with readily available mulch that does wonders for weed prevention and keeps our soil covered up, minimising moisture lost into the atmosphere and resulting in less water being used all round. We farm this way not because it is easy but because it is the only way that makes sense to us. It is our biggest form of rebellion.

Luckily, when it comes to soil, we couldn't get any better than our basalt base-rock soil at Boon Luck Farm. A lovely shade of terracotta and a lush loam, sometimes it just feels like we are cheating, starting off with such wonderful organic matter that we can only build upon (although the land was used for cattle for a long time, the damage that this caused has been reversed in the three years since we started). We are at the base of a chain of redundant volcanic mountains close to the coast – it is a microclimate that has a year-long growing season. On our farm we experiment with growing perennial and annual tropical and subtropical climate crops, though we also try our hand at low-chill cultivar temperate climate perennials as well as every single vegetable that will seed and, of course, red holy basil – loads of it. It is an Eden of sorts.

Now if you ask me why we continue to do this, I'd say it is to be an active part of that community of farmers who cannot imagine handing over control of their health to someone else, though by lucky coincidence what we also gain is immensely flavourful produce for our restaurants.

Bamboo Shoots

FAMILY
POACEAE

SPECIES
NASTUS ELATUS

CULTIVAR
NEW GUINEA GREEN

A giant grass, bamboo is the world's fastest-growing woody plant and can be used for anything from paper or clothing production to acting as a building material to make flooring, benchtops and fences. An environmentally sound choice (known to produce up to thirty-five per cent more oxygen than trees, as well as absorbing considerably more carbon dioxide), of the 1500 bamboo species in the world, about 110 are recorded to have edible shoots. These are an important food source in many Asian countries, with Thailand, China and Japan being the biggest consumers. —— Bamboo grows in a short but vigorous spurt during summer, with the new shoots emerging from the ground and reaching full height within a period of two to three months. While most of these bamboo shoots must be carefully prepared and blanched in boiling water before being consumed in order to remove potentially dangerous quantities of the natural plant toxins cyanogenic glycosides, *Nastus elatus* (or 'New Guinea Green') is the only variety that can be eaten from the ground without cooking. An attractive species with delicate, arching green-grey foliage and canes reaching up to 12 m (40 ft) tall, the shoots are deliciously sweet with a crisp yet tender texture. —— The New Guinea Green shoots that I source for my restaurants come from the Byron Bay area in northern New South Wales, with the temperate climate and high rainfall there seeming especially suited to this variety. The fact that you don't have to blanch or boil this particular bamboo shoot makes it extremely attractive from a culinary point of view; you can simply split the shoot in half and peel back the outer leaves to expose the tender inner core, then thinly slice it and serve it raw in a salad (though they are equally delicious grilled or blanched for a few seconds and brushed with butter).

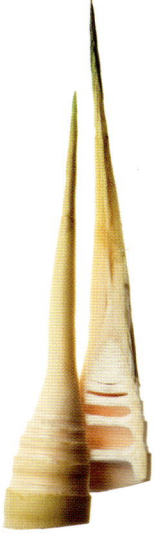

Peter Gilmore

BAMBOO SHOOTS, FERMENTED SHIITAKE CHAWANMUSHI, SMOKED PIG'S TROTTER BROTH

SERVES 8

Seasonal bamboo shoots are a textural treat. Here, they are combined with a delicate yet powerful fermented mushroom *chawanmushi* (savoury custard), crisp Jerusalem artichoke and a smoked pig's trotter broth. I love the fact that the bamboo is the main ingredient here – with the meat component taking on the form of the supporting light broth – rather than being the garnish to the meat dish, as you would typically expect.

NOTE: *The pig's trotter broth can be made in advance – it will keep refrigerated for 2–3 days or can be frozen for up to 6 months. If you don't have a cold smoking set-up at home, ask your butcher if he can smoke the trotters for you.*

SMOKED PIG'S TROTTER BROTH

1 onion, diced
1 carrot, diced
80 g (2¾ oz) unsalted butter
1.5 kg (3 lb 5 oz) chicken wings, halved
1.5 kg (3 lb 5 oz) cold-smoked pig's trotters, cut into pieces
200 ml (7 fl oz) oloroso sherry
3 litres (101 fl oz/12 cups) Chicken Stock (see Basics, page 240)
4 egg whites
4 jamón slices
8 g (¼ oz) dried shiitake mushrooms
1 x 5 cm (2 in) square dried kombu seaweed
½ chicken breast

In a 10 litre (340 fl oz) heavy-based stockpot, sauté the onion and carrot in the butter until softened. Add the chicken wings and lightly brown on all sides, then add the pig's trotters and sauté for a further 2 minutes. Deglaze the pot with the sherry, pour over the chicken stock and simmer gently for 5 hours, or until the liquid has reduced by about half. Strain the stock, discarding the solids and cleaning out the pot, then return the stock to the cleaned pot and leave it to cool.

Blitz together the egg whites, jamón, dried shiitake mushrooms, seaweed and chicken breast in a food processor to combine. Transfer the mixture to the pot with the cooled stock and bring to a very gentle simmer over a low heat. Simmer for 30 minutes to clarify, then strain the broth through a fine-mesh sieve and transfer it to a separate saucepan set over a high heat. Bring the broth to the boil and simmer until reduced by half, about 20 minutes. Strain through a fine muslin (cheesecloth) and set aside until needed.

FERMENTED SHIITAKE MUSHROOM JUICE

200 g (7 oz) shiitake mushrooms
1½ teaspoons sea salt

Finely slice the shiitake mushrooms and place in a vacuum-seal bag. Sprinkle over the salt, seal the bag, removing all the air, and leave at room temperature for 24 hours.

The next day, strain the mushrooms and gently squeeze them as dry as possible, reserving all the liquid. Refrigerate the liquid until needed (the mushrooms can be sautéed in butter to make a separate dish).

JERUSALEM ARTICHOKE CRISPS

4 Jerusalem artichokes
200 ml (7 fl oz) grapeseed oil

Steam the Jerusalem artichokes in a steamer set over boiling water for 15–20 minutes until tender. Leave the artichokes to cool, then cut them in half, carefully peeling the skin away from the flesh to leave the skins as whole and intact as possible. Spread the skins out on a chopping board and gently scape away any excess flesh. Heat the grapeseed oil to 180°C (350°F) and fry the skins until they are crisp and golden brown. Drain the skins on paper towel and keep them in a warm place until ready to serve.

FERMENTED MUSHROOM CHAWANMUSHI

4 eggs
360 ml (12 fl oz) milk
3 tablespoons Fermented Shiitake Mushroom Juice (see left)

Whisk all the ingredients together very well, then strain through a muslin (cheesecloth). Divide the mixture evenly among eight 175 ml (6 fl oz) ceramic dariole moulds, cover each tightly with plastic wrap and place in an 80°C (175°F) steamer for 13–15 minutes, or until the custard is just set.

To serve

12 New Guinea Green bamboo shoots, cut in half lengthways and outer leaves removed
100 ml (3½ fl oz) melted butter
sea salt

Bring a saucepan of salted water to the boil. In a separate saucepan, warm 200 ml (7 fl oz) of the smoked pig's trotter broth (freeze the excess and use it in soups as a base stock).

Blanch the halved bamboo shoots in the boiling water for 20 seconds. Drain, then brush with the melted butter and season with sea salt.

Spoon the custards out into individual serving bowls. Place three bamboo halves over each custard, add a tablespoon of the broth to each bowl and garnish with the crisp Jerusalem artichoke skins. Serve.

Snake Bean

FAMILY
FABACEAE

SPECIES
VIGNA UNGUICULATA* SUBSP. *SESQUIPEDALIS

CULTIVAR
CHINESE RED NOODLE

Originating in southern Asia, snake beans – also known as 'long' or 'yard-long' beans – may look like extra-long common beans, however they are actually a subspecies of cowpea (*Vigna unguiculata*). There are several varieties available, with most having green pods containing white, black or red seeds (though it is the tender, crunchy pods themselves that are generally consumed). The Chinese Red Noodle is one of the more stunning cultivars to be found, with a rich burgundy-coloured skin that doesn't fade much with cooking. —— Members of the *Fabaceae* family and true legumes, snake beans enrich the soil by fixing atmospheric nitrogen in nodules on their roots. The pods can grow to an impressive 50 cm (20 in) in length, though they are most often harvested at pencil thickness and about 40 cm (16 in). Growing on tall vines that can reach a height of about 3 m (10 ft), they are usually set on a twin flower, varying in colour from white and pink through to lavender depending on the variety. The beans require long, hot summers to do well and take a while to get going, with it taking two to three months from planting the seed until flowering commences, though from this point the pods themselves develop quickly – in fact, it can take as little as three to four days for an immature bean to grow to a length of 20 cm (8 in). They are very productive plants and picking the beans regularly encourages more to develop. During fruiting they require a good amount of water and they are tolerant of most soils. —— I love growing snake beans in my summer garden and the Chinese Red Noodle variety is visually dramatic, with its long red beans hanging from the vines like wind chimes. I prefer to pick the beans young, thinner than a pencil and at about 30 cm (12 in) in length, as I find they are more tender at this stage. Once harvested, they can be briefly blanched and buttered as you would young green beans, though in Asia they are mostly stir-fried or used raw in salads.

SALAD OF RED SNAKE BEANS
AND FRESH MUNTRIES

SERVES 8

Here I have used Chinese Red Noodle snake beans to make an Asian-inspired salad featuring textural ingredients such as pepitas, Chinese red dates and agretti alongside a uniquely Australian native fruit – the muntrie. Grown in southern Australia, muntries are a berry-like fruit that look like miniature apples and have a distinct flavour reminiscent of apple skin. If you struggle to find them, blueberries make an acceptable substitute.

1 tablespoon gochujang (Korean fermented red chilli paste)
2 tablespoons Japanese brown-rice vinegar
60 ml (2 fl oz/¼ cup) grapeseed oil
2 teaspoons cold-pressed sesame oil
16 Chinese Red Noodle snake beans (or other red snake beans),
trimmed and cut into 8 cm (3¼ in) lengths
2 small bunches of agretti, stems separated
150 g (5½ oz) fresh muntries, stems removed (or blueberries, if unavailable)
2 tablespoons pepitas (pumpkin seeds), lightly toasted
4 dried Chinese red dates, deseeded and julienned
sea salt

Combine the gochujang, rice vinegar, grapeseed oil and sesame oil in a bowl. Whisk together well to form a dressing and set aside until needed.

Have a bowl of iced water ready.

Bring a small saucepan of salted water to the boil. Blanch the snake beans in the boiling water for 30 seconds, then remove from the pan with a slotted spoon and refresh immediately in the iced water. Blanch the agretti stems for 10 seconds and transfer to the iced water to refresh.

Drain the blanched and refreshed vegetables and transfer to a large bowl. Add the muntries, pepitas and red date pieces, pour over the dressing and toss together well. Season with sea salt to taste and divide among serving bowls.

Palm Heart

FAMILY
ARECACEAE

SPECIES
BACTRIS GASIPAES

CULTIVAR
PEACH PALM

Palm heart is a vegetable traditionally consumed by indigenous populations in Central and South America and harvested from the core and growing bud of palm trees. One of the most famous is the coconut palm heart, the main ingredient in a salad referred to as millionaire's salad – the name linked to the fact that, traditionally, only wealthy people or island royalty could afford to buy a coconut palm tree just for its heart, as to harvest the heart is to kill the tree. —— Like the coconut palm, a lot of the traditionally cultivated palm species worldwide are from single-stemmed varieties, leading to their becoming threatened through over-harvesting. Fortunately, a number of palm species with edible hearts are clumping in nature, producing new suckers from the base of the older stems, which allows sustainable harvesting to occur. These include the peach palm, now the most widely grown commercial palm in Central and South America. In tropical conditions this is a fast-growing species that can be harvested from mature clumps every six to ten months without killing the tree. The peach palm has the added benefit of producing a heart resistant to oxidisation and browning following harvesting. Harvesting remains a very labour-intensive process, however, making fresh palm hearts a relatively expensive product. —— In Australia, there are a number of palm species that are edible and are considered to be native foods – these include species such the Alexander palm, bungalow palm and cabbage palm. At present, though, there is only one producer of peach palm hearts in Australia: the northern Queensland–based Palm Hearts Australia run by Yan and Heather Diczbalis. I have been buying palm hearts from Yan for the past ten years – I love palm heart's crisp texture and slightly nutty, young corn–like flavour. I tend to use palm heart thinly sliced and barely cooked as a textural ingredient in my food, although it can also be baked to accentuate its flavour.

PALM HEART CONGEE, SCALLOPS, BLACK VINEGAR LAVER

SERVES 8

Congee is a dish that has become a signature of mine, and one I've been cooking in various forms for the past fifteen years (one of Quay's more famous dishes is the mud crab congee, which appeared in my first book). This version features the unique texture of palm heart, along with sashimi scallops and a black vinegar seaweed dressing.

BASIC CONGEE

30 g (1 oz/3 tablespoons) fresh ginger, finely sliced
50 g (1¾ oz) finely sliced spring onion (scallion), white part only
4 teaspoons grapeseed oil
2 litres (68 fl oz/8 cups) Chicken Stock (see Basics, page 240)
160 g (5½ oz) Japanese crushed glutinous rice

Lightly sauté the ginger and spring onion in a saucepan together with the grapeseed oil until translucent. Add the chicken stock and simmer over a low heat for 15 minutes, then remove from the heat and leave to cool.

Strain the cooled stock, discarding the ginger and spring onion. Set aside 350 ml (12 fl oz) of the stock for the dressing and to serve (as right), then transfer 500 ml (17 fl oz/2 cups) of the remainder to a heavy-based saucepan set over a medium heat. Add the glutinous rice to the pan and cook for 30 minutes, stirring occasionally and adding more of the strained stock a ladleful or so at a time as it is absorbed by the rice, until the rice is cooked through and the congee has a thick, porridge-like consistency. Remove from the heat and set aside until needed.

BLACK VINEGAR LAVER DRESSING

½ sheet dried Korean laver seaweed
   (approx. 10 x 20 cm/4 x 8 in)
1 tablespoon good-quality black-rice vinegar
150 ml (5 fl oz) reserved infused chicken stock (as left)

Crush the dried seaweed sheet into small pieces. Add the black-rice vinegar and the reserved infused chicken stock to a small saucepan and bring to the boil, then immediately remove from the heat. Add the seaweed to the pan and set aside for at least 1 minute to allow it to infuse into the stock.

Additional ingredients

200 g (7 oz) palm heart core, cut into 1 mm (¹⁄₁₆-in) thick discs
sea salt
8 large sashimi-grade scallops, cut widthways into 6 slices

To serve

Gently reheat the congee, adding the remaining 200 ml (7 fl oz) of reserved infused chicken stock, then stir in the sliced palm heart and bring to the boil, stirring constantly. Season to taste with sea salt, adding a splash more stock to loosen up the congee to a porridge-like consistency, if required.

Divide the congee among warmed bowls and top with the scallop slices. Reheat the black vinegar laver dressing and drizzle a little over the top of each bowl. Serve immediately.

Asparagus Pea

FAMILY
FABACEAE

SPECIES
LOTUS TETRAGONOLOBUS

The asparagus pea is an annual legume endemic to the Mediterranean region, where it is a common spring-blooming wildflower (though records also exist of its cultivation in Sicily from the mid-16th century). It should not be confused with the much larger winged bean (*Psophocarpus tetragonolobus*, also known as the Goa bean), which is native to New Guinea and grown throughout Southeast Asia. —— The asparagus pea grows about 20 cm (8 in) tall with low, spreading branches spanning out around 40 cm (16 in) from the centre. Adaptable to most garden soils, it thrives in warmer climates and has the added benefit of fixing nitrogen into the soil. The plant has small trifoliate leaves and deep crimson flowers that are borne in pairs and which, like most beans and pea plants, are also edible. The pods that form after pollination are about 5 cm (2 in) in length and are lined with four small frills or 'wings'. —— The asparagus pea is a striking legume with a flavour somewhere between asparagus and peas, hence its common name. The peas are best harvested soon after they have formed, while they are young and tender, and are best prepared simply – cooked briefly in boiling salted water or steamed. They are delicious with just the simple addition of melted butter and sea salt. —— I grew the asparagus pea for the first time last season and must say it was one of the prettiest plants in my garden. The trick is to keep a close eye on it and harvest it regularly as the pods can become tough and woody if left on the plant for too long.

SALAD OF ASPARAGUS PEAS,
GREEN TEA AND KOMBU OIL, KAMPOT PEPPER

SERVES 8

Asparagus peas are one of those rare garden delicacies that require attention during the harvesting stage; they need picking soon after they emerge so they are sweet and tender and not too fibrous. Here, they are treated simply – briefly blanched, dressed with a fragrant oil and finished with their own blossoms and a hint of heat from the kampot pepper.

NOTE: *This recipe will yield more green tea and kombu oil than is needed. The excess can be stored in the refrigerator for a couple of weeks and used to brush over grilled fish or dress other salads.*

1 x 10 cm (4 in) square dried kombu seaweed
400 ml (13½ fl oz) grapeseed oil
1 tablespoon good-quality green tea leaves
1 teaspoon kampot peppercorns
2 teaspoons Korean roasted sea salt or regular sea salt
250 g (9 oz) asparagus peas
about 30 asparagus pea flowers

Place the seaweed in a bowl, cover with cold water and leave to soak for 1 hour.

Preheat the oven to 180°C (350°F).

Drain the rehydrated seaweed, place on a wire rack and roast in the oven for 20 minutes, or until lightly coloured and crispy. Remove from the oven and leave to cool completely, then break into small pieces.

Transfer the seaweed pieces to a blender together with the grapeseed oil and green tea leaves and blitz on high speed for 2 minutes. Leave the oil to infuse for at least 2 hours before straining through a fine muslin (cheesecloth) or coffee-filter bag, discarding the solids. Set aside until needed.

In a mortar and pestle, grind the kampot peppercorns to a fine powder, add the sea salt and mix together well. Set aside.

Bring a large saucepan of salted water to the boil and have a large bowl of iced water on standby. Blanch the asparagus peas in the boiling water for 30 seconds, then strain and immediately refresh in the iced water. Transfer the peas to a clean tea towel (dish towel) to drain.

To assemble the salad, place the drained asparagus peas in a large bowl together with 3 tablespoons of the green tea and kombu oil and mix together well. Season the dressed peas with the kampot pepper and salt mixture to taste, then divide among serving bowls. Serve garnished with the asparagus pea flowers.

Aztec Broccoli (Huauzontle)

FAMILY
CHENOPODIACEAE

SPECIES
CHENOPODIUM NUTTALLIAE

Also referred to as Aztec spinach or huauzontle, Aztec broccoli is a member of the *Chenopodium* species along with quinoa, true spinach, Good King Henry and Fat Hen. Native to Mexico, Aztec broccoli is grown for both its leaves and flower heads, which are picked before the flowers open and resemble tiny broccoli heads (hence the vegetable's common name). The taste, however, is different from broccoli – almost grassy and with a hint of spicy citrus. ——— In Mexico, Aztec broccoli is traditionally coated in an egg batter and deep-fried like a kind of fritter, though it also holds its crisp, crunchy texture after a brief blanching in boiling water and tastes delicious simply brushed with butter and sprinkled with sea salt. Like quinoa, Aztec broccoli's mature seed can also be harvested for food and, in some parts of Mexico, it is ground into a flour to make tortillas. ——— I have found Aztec broccoli to grow quickly, taking about six weeks from seed, with the green leaves developing a purple tinge that makes it an attractive plant in the garden. While I grew my crop in spring, I imagine it would also grow well in autumn (it may bolt to seed too quickly in summer).

PIPPIES, XO, AZTEC BROCCOLI

SERVES 8

Aztec broccoli, or huauzontle, is the perfect foil for this dish of lightly steamed pippies – it has a spicy note that stands up well to the complex flavour and heat of the XO sauce. The pippies here can be substituted for any type of clam – or even mussels – and though the XO sauce takes a while to make, the flavour is well worth the effort.

BASIC STOCK

100 ml (3½ fl oz) grapeseed oil
1 kg (2 lb 3 oz) chicken wings
1 large snapper head or other fish head
1 small brown onion, chopped
1 inner celery stalk, white part only
½ carrot, chopped
200 g (7 oz) squid trimmings
150 ml (5 fl oz) unoaked chardonnay
2.5 litres (85 fl oz/10 cups) cold water
250 g (9 oz) pippies (vongole) or other clams

Heat the oil in a stockpot over a medium–high heat, add the chicken wings and snapper head and cook, turning occasionally, for 5 minutes or until golden brown all over. Add the vegetables and squid and continue to cook for 2 minutes, or until the vegetables and squid are lightly browned. Deglaze the pot with the wine and reduce until evaporated, then add the water. Skim off the fat from the surface and simmer over a low heat for 2½ hours, or until reduced by half. Add the pippies to the pot and simmer for a further 30 minutes, then strain the stock through a fine-mesh sieve, discarding the solids. Transfer to a suitable container and refrigerate until needed (it will keep for up to 2 days).

XO SAUCE

150 ml (5 fl oz) grapeseed oil
60 g (2 oz) fresh ginger, finely grated
60 g (2 oz) garlic, finely grated
40 g (1½ oz) mild Korean red chilli flakes
25 g (1 oz) dried scallops
50 g (1¾ oz) dried jamón, sliced
50 g (1¾ oz) dried shiitake mushrooms
150 ml (5 fl oz) oloroso sherry
100 ml (3½ fl oz) Japanese brown-rice vinegar
1.5 litres (51 fl oz/6 cups) Basic Stock (see left)
500 ml (17 fl oz/2 cups) water
30 g (1 oz) unsalted butter
1 x 5 cm (2 in) square dried kombu seaweed
½ teaspoon xantana (fermented cornstarch)
sea salt

Heat the grapeseed oil in a stockpot over a medium heat. Add the ginger, garlic and chilli flakes and cook, stirring, until the ginger and garlic have softened. Add the dried scallops, jamón and shiitake mushrooms and sauté for 2 minutes. Increase the heat to high, deglaze with the sherry and brown-rice vinegar and reduce until the liquid has evaporated by half. Add the basic stock, water and butter, bring to a very gentle simmer and cook for 1 hour, then add the kombu square, remove the pot from the heat and leave to infuse for a further 1 hour. Strain through a medium-mesh sieve, lightly pressing on the solids in the sieve with the back of a spoon or ladle to extract the liquid and allow some of the solids through. Transfer the sauce to a clean saucepan and return to a simmer, then whisk in the xantana until smooth and slightly thickened. Season to taste with salt and set aside until needed (it will keep in the refrigerator for up to 2 days).

Additional ingredients

2 kg (4 lb 6 oz) pippies (vongole) or other clams
4 leafy Aztec broccoli heads, broken into florets and leaves

To serve

Warm the XO sauce in a saucepan. Add the pippies to a steamer basket set over simmering water and steam until opened. Remove the meat from the shells, discarding the shells along with any pippies that haven't opened, and stir it through the XO sauce. Meanwhile, blanch the Aztec broccoli in a separate saucepan of boiling water for 30 seconds. Drain.

Divide the pippies and sauce among warmed serving bowls and top with the Aztec broccoli.

Minutina (Buck's Horn)

FAMILY
PLANTAGINACEAE

SPECIES
PLANTAGO CORONOPUS

Minutina, also known as erba stella and buck's horn plantain, is native to Eurasia and North Africa but treasured in Italy as a unique Italian heirloom, where it has been regarded as a cultivated vegetable since 1586. It is a widely used ingredient in *misticanza*, the Italian salad mixture of wild and cultivated leaves, which originated in the Marche region of Italy. —— An annual vegetable, minutina grows to about 25 cm (10 in) and produces rosettes of unique long green leaves, which have a succulent and juicy yet crunchy texture and a wonderful, nutty flavour. The leaves can be harvested as required but are best when young before the plant flowers, as the flowers draw up many of the essential oils from the leaves (the flowers are also edible). Minutina is very adaptable to any soil type, although it does require good drainage and to be watered well in order to maintain the succulence of its tender leaves. Generally grown as an autumn or winter crop, it will tolerate cold weather but not heavy snows. In the wild it prefers coastal regions, so will tolerate saline soils and sea spray. ——The English name for minutina, buck's horn, refers to the forked antler-like tips of the leaves that give the plant its unique appearance. While it is this that first attracted me to growing minutina, its distinctive texture and sweet grass-like nuttiness are the reasons I will continue to do so. You can treat minutina as you would young spinach leaves; its qualities lend themselves well to being paired with seafood dishes, while its vibrant green colour and sweet flavour become even more prominent when briefly blanched.

ROASTED NORI UDON, WILTED MINUTINA, STAG SEAWEED

This dish developed naturally; wilted minutina's seagrass-like appearance led me to thoughts of pairing it with seaweed for visual effect, while the vegetable's textural qualities work well with those of the udon noodles. The dish is then finished with a liquid produced from the fermentation of cabbage and seaweed, with the addition of brown butter to round out the flavour.

NOTE: *The salting of the cabbage and seaweed for the ferment needs to be started 5 days in advance of cooking, while the nori seaweed sheets for the noodles require dehydrating overnight.*

CABBAGE AND NORI FERMENT

200 g (7 oz) hispi or napa-style cabbage, leaves separated
1 sheet nori seaweed, toasted
1 teaspoon sea salt

Add the cabbage leaves and nori seaweed sheet to a large vacuum-seal bag, sprinkle over the salt and seal the bag, removing all the air. Leave the bag at room temperature for 5 days to allow the cabbage and seaweed to ferment naturally. After 5 days, remove the cabbage leaves and nori sheet from the bag, discarding any liquid, then juice using an electric juicer. Pass the juice through a fine-mesh sieve, measure 200 ml (7 fl oz) into an airtight container and refrigerate until needed.

NORI UDON NOODLES

2 sheets nori seaweed
500 g (1 lb 2 oz/3⅓ cups) strong wheat flour
260 ml (9 fl oz) filtered water
40 g (1½ oz) salt
50 g (1¾ oz) rice flour

Dehydrate the nori seaweed sheets overnight in a dehydrator or a very low oven preheated to 50°C (120°F) until crisp, then blend to a powder in a spice grinder. Measure out 7 g (¼ oz) of the powder, transfer to a food processor together with the flour and blitz briefly until well incorporated.

Add the water and salt to a bowl and whisk together well until the salt has completely dissolved. Place the nori flour mixture in a separate bowl and, using your fingers, slowly mix in the salted water little by little to form a dough. Once all the water has been added, bring the dough together in a loose ball, cover with plastic wrap and leave to rest for 30 minutes.

Once rested, transfer the dough to an electric mixer with the hook attachment attached and mix on the lowest speed for 20 minutes, or until the dough is smooth and elastic. Reform the dough into a ball, cover again with plastic wrap and leave to rest for another 1 hour, then roll the dough through a pasta machine to a thickness of 2 mm (¹/₁₆ in) and cut into 2 mm x 15 cm (¹/₁₆ x 6 in) noodles. Dust the noodles generously with the rice flour to prevent them from sticking together and refrigerate until needed.

Additional ingredients

sea salt
200 ml (7 fl oz) Brown Butter (see Basics, page 241)
2 bunches of minutina (approx. 100 g/3½ oz),
    leaves separated and rinsed
50 ml (1¾ fl oz) melted butter
about 30 fresh stag seaweed fronds (optional)

To serve

Place two saucepans of water on the stove, season one with sea salt and bring both to the boil.

Meanwhile, add the fermented cabbage and nori juice to a small heavy-based saucepan with the brown butter. Bring to the boil, whisking occasionally, and simmer for 5 minutes, or until reduced by half. Set aside.

Add the chilled udon noodles to the pan with the non-salted water and cook for 90 seconds. Drain and transfer to a bowl.

Blanch the minutina in the boiling salted water for 15 seconds. Drain well, then brush with the melted butter and season lightly with sea salt.

Pour the reduced fermented cabbage, nori and brown butter liquid over the drained udon noodles and mix together well, then fold through the dressed minutina. Divide the minutina and noodles among warmed serving bowls and garnish with fresh stag seaweed, if using. Serve.

Daylily

FAMILY
ASPHODELACEAE

SPECIES
HEMEROCALLIS LILIOASPHODELUS

CULTIVAR
MALENY MARDI GRAS

Not to be confused with true lilies (which are inedible), daylilies have been used in cooking for centuries. The genus name *Hemerocallis* is derived from the Greek words *hemera* meaning day and *kallos* meaning beauty – an appropriate name since each flower only blooms for a single day. —— Daylilies are a truly beautiful addition to any garden and there are now literally thousands of cultivars available in an amazing range of colours from the traditional yellows through to vibrant reds, purples, oranges and near whites along with multi-coloured blossoms. Other features that have been developed and hybridised include ruffled edges, differently sized flowers and varieties that will flower twice a year. —— Most daylilies bloom in early summer, with multiple buds on each plant meaning that even though a flower will only last a day, there is every chance a new flower will be ready to open the next day. Each variety will flower for between three to four weeks, so if you plant multiple varieties you can have flowers through most of the summer (some of the newer varieties will also give you a second flush in the autumn). They are very tolerant plants that cope well with drought and adapt well to most soils and conditions, preferring a sunny position. Every third year they can be dug up and divided; it is best to do this at the very beginning of spring. Treated this way, daylilies are a long-lived perennial plant. —— Besides their beauty, the added bonus with daylilies is that they are delicious. Picked fresh in the morning as they open, the petals make a delicious, colourful addition to salads; I find the flavour is very similar to sweet cooked leeks. You can also choose to harvest the daylily buds just before they are ready to open, then dehydrate and preserve them for later use as they do in Chinese cuisine (the Chinese refer to the dried buds as 'golden needles' and generally rehydrate them in warm water for use in stir-fries and soups). Some varieties of daylily produce swollen rhizomes that are also edible, and I have also found that sautéing fresh buds or individual opened petals in butter makes a delicious and vibrant accompaniment to a dish. Although a flower isn't traditionally considered a vegetable, the flavour and texture of daylilies means they should not be considered a mere garnish, but rather a welcome addition to any vegetable garden.

WILTED DAYLILIES, SEA URCHIN, KOSHIHIKARI RICE, SALTED EGG YOLK

SERVES 8

In this recipe the daylilies are not simply a garnish, as often is the case with flowers. Here, the petals are treated as a vegetable and a central component of the dish. The daylily's beautiful rich orange colour complements that of the urchin, while its sweet flavour – reminiscent of sautéed leeks – counterbalances the dish's briny notes.

SALT-CURED EGG YOLKS

approx. 120 g (4½ oz) sea salt flakes
2 eggs

In the base of a small ceramic bowl, lay a bed of sea salt about 3 cm (1¼ in) deep and wide enough to hold two egg yolks slightly apart. Make two small egg yolk-shaped indentations in the salt. Crack the eggs and carefully remove the yolks, then place the yolks in the salt indentations. Carefully cover each yolk with a mound of the remaining sea salt, then cover the bowl with plastic wrap and refrigerate for 7 days.

SEA URCHIN BUTTER

150 g (5½ oz) unsalted butter
80 g (2¾ oz) fresh sea urchin roe
sea salt

Dice the butter, transfer to a bowl and leave to soften to room temperature, then add the sea urchin and whisk together well. Pass the sea urchin butter through a fine-mesh sieve, season to taste with salt and refrigerate until needed.

To serve

120 g (4½ oz) koshihikari rice, washed
2 teaspoons ume vinegar or rice vinegar
100 ml (3½ fl oz) Chicken Stock (see Basics, page 240)
16 sea urchin roes
about 40 daylily petals
50 ml (1¾ fl oz) melted butter
sea salt

Remove the cured egg yolks from their salt bed and brush off any excess salt (the egg yolks should be firm to the touch). Remove the sea urchin butter from the fridge, cut it into dice and leave to return to room temperature.

Cook the koshihikari rice in a rice cooker until tender (alternatively, add it to a saucepan with 180 ml/6 fl oz boiling water and cook using the classic absorption method). Once the rice is cooked, stir through the ume or rice vinegar, then transfer to a medium-sized saucepan together with the chicken stock and sea urchin butter. Heat the rice, stirring well, until all the butter has melted and is fully incorporated (it should have the appearance of classic risotto), then remove from the heat and immediately fold through the sea urchin roes. Season to taste, and keep warm.

Blanch the daylily petals in a saucepan of boiling water for 5 seconds, then drain and pat dry with paper towel. Transfer to a large bowl or plate, brush generously with the melted butter and season to taste with sea salt.

To serve, place a large spoonful of rice on each serving plate. Garnish with the wilted daylilies and finely grate some salted egg yolk over each dish to finish.

ERIKA WATSON AND HAYDEN DRUCE

EPICUREAN HARVEST

I first met Erika and Hayden a few years ago while they were working on Beridale Farm, which was then owned by Richard and Nina Kalina (Richard and Nina were the first growers willing to produce bespoke heirloom and rare vegetables for me at Quay back in 2006). Richard and Nina sold their farm in 2013, however Erika and Hayden eventually leased the 1 acre vegetable plot from the new owners and kept producing wonderful organic vegetables for me at Quay.

Erika and Hayden write –

Epicurean Harvest began with a relationship between a couple of landowners, a couple of chefs, and us – Erika and Hayden. Having both finished a rigourous four-year applied degree in horticultural science – which had given us an in-depth understanding of the science behind plant physiology, soil biology and climate – we started by leasing a 1 acre block in the Upper Blue Mountains west of Sydney after developing a good relationship with the land owners, holding steadfast to our beliefs in remaining transparent, accountable and honest to both the land and the people who took our produce. Both of us are full-time organic vegetable growers and in the three years leasing and supplying more and more restaurants in Sydney and the local area, we managed to save enough for a loan and bought 120 acres in Hartley, New South Wales, which we named Bula Mirri. The aim in owning land was to have greater influence on the land management decisions surrounding the market garden.

Like a great percentage of Australia, Hartley is a seasonally dry environment. We need to manage this, which requires using farming methods to reduce run-off and evaporation. Understanding the different cycles that occur across the landscape and balancing those cycles to improve biodiversity and ground cover in the entire ecosystem is fundamental.

In managing the market garden, we aim to take actions that look after the soil we rely on. The soil is our livelihood and it is fragile, and many of the tools we have at our disposal are capable of creating harm very easily. In our market garden we follow a relatively simple but effective procedure for soil health management. We incorporate green manures, crop rotation and mulching into our planning to help feed the soil biology routinely; we use compost, compost teas, worm leachate and castings as added food and tonic for soil conditioning; and we use a tarping method with silage tarps to increase the rate of decomposition of organic matter and to provide a bed in which we can then easily plant the next crop. Green manures and mulching are both different forms of ground cover that reduce the exposure of bare soil to the sun and elements. They are also both sources of organic matter that can be broken down by the soil biology to cycle nutrients and provide healthy soil that can hold water more effectively, releasing nutrients as the plants require them.

The seeds and varieties of plants we choose to grow have a range of requirements: flavour, appearance, reliability and productivity. Within the market garden we have both heirloom/heritage seed and hybrid varieties. Heirloom/heritage refers to the seed being open-pollinated, resulting in the crossing of diverse genetics, and the seed from that crossing will grow and express the dominant genes. This is a traditional plant-breeding method, which allows for seed saving to be tailored to provenance, increasing resilience over time to its growing environment. A common trade-off is that the crops from heirloom seed can be variable in all of the desired requirements mentioned above – sometimes better, sometimes worse. It is important to aid in the saving of heirloom seed and the proliferation of genetics as, without them, diversity could be lost forever. It is difficult for market gardeners to save seed of open pollinated varieties when they also need to focus on a range of vegetables for consumption. It becomes very complex to manage for both the seed and space needed to allow it to grow out while still incorporating soil health management and crop rotations seasonally. Most market gardeners participate in seed saving to some degree, but balance it with common hybrid varieties that also meet the desired requirements.

Hybrid refers to seed produced from two known parent types that will express consistent, uniform genetics. This is a modern form of plant breeding, and it can take many years of research and development to produce what are often called the F1 hybrids. They can be as flavoursome and beautiful as the heirloom, but are very often also consistent in productivity and reliability. They can also have the genetics from their selected parent types to resist other environmental pressures, like bolting in hot weather or early flowering at the start of spring, and can be sourced as organic seed. The trade-off for F1 hybrids is the saved seed from them cannot be bred or used to produce the same crop; they are therefore often owned by seed companies and have little provenance. Sadly, F1 hybrids in current food systems are often bred for ease of logistics and transport, instead of flavour and eating quality. This is to meet the demand from large centralised markets and consumers for appearance, reliability and productivity. Like many market gardeners, we select F1 hybrids that are true to our requirements, as we do not want to compromise flavour and eating quality but also need to earn our living by producing food reliably.

We are honest and transparent with what we can achieve saving heirloom seed and there is trust in the hybrids we grow to meet the demands of the menus and eating quality. The chefs we work with respect the value and cost to us in producing heirlooms and this allows them to be showcased to the consumer. We can all be inspired by the skills of a good chef and equally amazing producers. The two together, though, turn this inspiration into a story that feeds culture and the belly, and helps people better understand where their food comes from.

We have been custodians of Bula Mirri since September 2016, and our goal for the farm is to help sustain our organic market garden, Epicurean Harvest, as well as foster and support other regenerative enterprises: a place for the interaction of art, creativity, food, agriculture and ecology to be diverse, open and exciting. We want to continue our close relationships with chefs to bring all of these ideas to a greater audience. Eating is an act of farming, and together growers, chefs and consumers alike need to keep challenging the conventional paradigm.

Precoce di Jesi Cauliflower

FAMILY
BRASSICACEAE

SPECIES
BRASSICA OLERACEA VAR. **BOTRYTIS**

CULTIVAR
PRECOCE DI JESI

Precoce di Jesi is a rare heirloom variety of cauliflower originally grown near Venice. It has a circular shape with a soft yellow colour and spiralling florets. —— Cauliflowers in general are thought to have been cultivated for more than 2000 years in the eastern Mediterranean region. Closely related to cabbage, broccoli and other brassicas, they are appreciated for their tightly clustered curds (usually white to cream in colour, though there are varieties that are purple and green), mild flavour and versatility in the kitchen. Cauliflowers contain high levels of the antioxidant glucoraphanin, a compound said to reduce blood cholesterol and the risk of cancer. —— Cauliflowers are best grown in full sun in an organically rich, fertile soil that is both well composted and well drained. Spring and autumn temperatures suit them best, and varieties like Precoce di Jesi have been developed that are 'early' – meaning they are planted in early spring and harvested in early summer. They do not do well in the heat of summer, though there are varieties that give an autumn harvest, as well as others that can be sown in late summer and 'over-wintered' to produce an early spring crop. —— I first came across the Precoce di Jesi in an Italian seed catalogue and knew I had to grow it, initially for its beautiful pale yellow colour and spiralling florets. Now I continue to grow it for its flavour and tenderness. One of my favourite ways to prepare it is as an Indian-style pakora, coating the cauliflower in a spiced batter made from chickpea flour before frying, though it also makes a delicious purée or soup and pairs with shellfish beautifully.

PRECOCE DI JESI, PORK CRACKLING AND AGED COMTÉ SALAD

SERVES 8

Precoce di Jesi is my favourite cauliflower; the yellow heads and green stems make it visually striking and it has a clean, sweet flavour. In this salad, I have combined it with pork crackling and aged comté, though you could easily make this vegetarian by replacing the pork crackling with sourdough croutons.

PORK CRACKLING

1 x 300 g (10½ oz) piece pork skin
1 litre (34 fl oz/4 cups) grapeseed oil

Place the pork skin in a vacuum-seal bag and seal, removing all the air. Steam on high for 2 hours, then cool and remove the skin from the bag. Place the skin, underside up, on a chopping board and scrape away as much fat as possible using a sharp knife. Transfer the skin to a dehydrator or a very low oven preheated to 80°C (175°F) and dehydrate for 4 hours, or until dry and crisp.

In a large heavy-based saucepan, heat the oil to 200°C (400°F). Add the dried skin pieces to the hot oil in three or four batches – they should instantaneously puff up and triple in size. Remove from the oil, drain well on paper towel and leave to cool, then break into small shards and store in an airtight container until required.

WHITE CAULIFLOWER PURÉE

1 tablespoon finely diced shallot
1 teaspoon finely diced garlic
50 g (1¾ oz) unsalted butter
200 g (7 oz) white cauliflower florets, finely chopped
250 ml (8½ fl oz/1 cup) Chicken Stock (see Basics, page 240)
50 g (1¾ oz) crème fraîche
sea salt

In a heavy-based saucepan, sauté the shallots and garlic in the butter over a medium heat until translucent. Increase the heat to high, add the cauliflower florets and chicken stock and simmer until virtually all the liquid has evaporated, then transfer the mixture to a food processor and blend on high speed to a fine purée. Pass through a fine-mesh sieve and leave to cool completely, then whisk in the crème fraîche and season with sea salt. Refrigerate until needed.

CHAMOMILE VINAIGRETTE

¼ teaspoon dried chamomile flowers
1 tablespoon lemon juice
1 teaspoon finely diced shallots
3 tablespoons extra-virgin olive oil

Whisk together all the ingredients in a small bowl.

Additional ingredients

1 Precoce di Jesi cauliflower head, cut into very small florets
sea salt
100 g (3½ oz) aged comté
1 small handful of fresh chamomile flowers or other small edible white flowers

To serve

Bring a large saucepan of salted water to the boil and have a large bowl of iced water on standby. Blanch the cauliflower florets in the boiling water for 10 seconds, then immediately refresh in the iced water. Drain.

Dress the blanched cauliflower florets in the chamomile vinaigrette and season to taste with sea salt, then arrange the dressed cauliflower on a platter. Using a microplane, grate over the comté. Top with the pork crackling pieces and small dots of cauliflower purée, and garnish with chamomile or other white flowers. Serve.

Rosa Bianca Eggplant

FAMILY
SOLANACEAE

SPECIES
SOLANUM MELONGENA

CULTIVAR
ROSA BIANCA

The variety of sizes, shapes and colours of cultivated eggplants is astonishing – from the familiar large, elongated dark purple-skinned varieties familiar in the West, to the long slender green-skinned and apple eggplants of Thailand, not to mention the beautiful mauve and white variegated varieties of Italy, the orange-skinned Turkish varieties or the wonderful large, black flat-bottomed Kamo eggplants of Japan. Indeed, the name 'eggplant' itself most likely developed from the white-skinned varieties, originally grown as ornamentals, which have the shape and size of a duck's egg. ——— The culinary uses for eggplants are every bit as varied as the countries they are grown in. Their sponge-like flesh, which readily absorbs flavour, lends them an incredible versatility that is demonstrated in the curries and relishes of India, the smoky Arabic babaganoush, the grilled antipasto of Italy, the baked Greek moussaka and the slow-braised dishes of Japan, to name but a few. ——— The Rosa Bianca eggplant is a strikingly beautiful cultivar from Italy with mottled mauve and white skin. The flesh of this particular eggplant is white with very few seeds and almost no bitterness. It is a great variety to grow, particularly in warmer climates, where it generally takes around three months from seedling to maturity. I have found it to produce extremely large fruit, so it is a good idea to stake your plants as you would a tomato bush. I have also found it useful to increase the yield by hand-pollinating the flowers, as bees are not as attracted to eggplant flowers as they are to other flowers in the garden. The Rosa Bianca is one of my favourite vegetables to grow – seeing the mauve and white fruit begin to develop and lend the summer vegetable garden their exotic splash of colour is always exciting.

Peter Gilmore

CRISPY SICILIAN-INSPIRED
ROSA BIANCA EGGPLANT

SERVES 8

This dish takes inspiration from two very distinct cooking traditions. Half of it is inspired by a Schezuan eggplant dish that is served with a hot, sweet sauce containing chillies, Schezuan peppers and vinegar, and which has an extremely crisp batter. The other half – the sweet Sicilian-style garnish of pistachio nuts, lemon and currants – comes from one of the many eggplant dishes of Italy.

750 ml (25½ fl oz/3 cups) chilled soda water (club soda)
2 teaspoons xantana (fermented cornstarch)
100 g (3½ oz) rice flour
150 g (5½ oz) tapioca flour
1 whole lemon
1.5 litres (51 fl oz/6 cups) grapeseed or sunflower oil
1 x Sherry Caramel (see page 18)
50 g (1¾ oz) currants
50 g (1¾ oz) shelled pistachio nuts, halved
1 large Rosa Bianca eggplant
sea salt

To make the batter, pour the chilled soda water into a tall stainless steel or plastic cylinder container large enough to insert a hand-held blender. Add the xantana and blend well, then add the rice flour and 100 g (3½ oz) of the tapioca flour and continue to blend to form a smooth batter. Refrigerate until needed.

Bring a large saucepan of water to the boil, add the lemon and boil for 2 minutes. Drain, then re-fill the saucepan with water and repeat the process twice more – this will soften the lemon and extract some of its harsher flavours. Let the lemon cool completely, then cut into quarters with a sharp knife, remove and discard the flesh and seeds and cut the skin into 2 mm (⅛ in) cubes.

In a large heavy-based saucepan, heat the grapeseed oil to 190°C (375°F). In a separate saucepan, warm the sherry caramel together with the currants, lemon skin pieces and pistachios.

Cut the eggplant lengthways into 3 cm (1¼ in) thick slices, then cut each slice in half. Lightly dust the eggplant in the remaining tapioca flour, then add to the bowl with the prepared batter and turn to coat well. Add the battered eggplant to the hot oil in small batches and deep-fry for 4 minutes, turning, or until golden brown. Drain on paper towel and season well with sea salt.

Divide the fried eggplant pieces among serving plates, drizzle over the warm caramel dressing and serve immediately.

Umbrian Wild Pea (Roveja)

FAMILY
FABACEAE

SPECIES
PISUM SATIVUM* SUBSP. *ARVENSE

CULTIVAR
ROVEJA DI CASTELLUCCIO

The Umbrian wild pea, also known as the roveja, is a small, pea-like legume with colours that vary from dark green to grey and brown, some with speckling. It was first cultivated by Neolithic people living on a plain in the Sibillini mountains, a mountain range that covers the south-eastern area of Umbria and an area that archaeological finds suggest may have been the first inhabited part of what is now Italy. The Umbrian wild pea is believed by some researchers to be an ancestor of the common pea, though others claim it to be a true species – either way, its botanical classification is still unclear. —— In past centuries, the roveja was a staple in the diet of the herders and farmers who lived on the mountains and was eaten in the form of a *puls*, an Ancient Roman style of porridge. Though still consumed in the Middle Ages, over time the roveja was forgotten, its demise caused by the tough, labour-intensive harvesting it required on difficult, high-altitude land. By the 1990s only a few locals remembered the roveja. Thankfully, on finding some plants growing in gullies near streams, some of those locals decided to take action. Daniele Testa explains, 'Like my father before me, we were growing heritage crops here. My brother and I decided to start re-cultivating the roveja. When we applied for organic certification, the people in Brussels and the wider EU couldn't believe this plant was the real thing'. Another two women from Civita di Cascia, Silvana Cresci and Gertrude Moretti, also began to reassess this rare legume. By the end of the 1990s in Italy, the Universities of Perugia and Ancona, along with local action groups and several farmers, had started to experiment and resume production and, by 2006, the roveja came under the protection of the Slow Food Foundation. —— I first came across this pea in 2015 while I was visiting Milan, and its unique look with its multitude of colours really intrigued me. After soaking and a long, gentle slow cook, the roveja holds its shape without breaking up and its texture is very satisfying. The flavour is more like that of dried beans or lentils than peas. It's crazy to think that this ancient vegetable could have been lost to history were it not for a few passionate people who saw its special value.

SLOW-BRAISED UMBRIAN WILD PEAS, FERMENTED MUSHROOM AND BLACK GARLIC PURÉE

SERVES 8

In Umbria these peas are traditionally slow-braised or ground into a powder to make a type of polenta. They have an extraordinary depth of flavour, and the dried variety can be used anywhere you would use a high-quality dried bean. In this dish – perfect for serving over a piece of slowly braised meat – I have enhanced their flavour by braising them in an oxtail broth, though a meat-free version made with vegetable stock would also be delicious. Cold-smoking the oxtail is optional, though it does impart a lovely flavour.

NOTE: *Both the soaking of the peas and the salting of the shiitake mushrooms for the fermented mushroom and black garlic purée need to be done a day in advance of cooking.*

FERMENTED MUSHROOM AND BLACK GARLIC PURÉE

300 g (10½ oz) shiitake mushrooms
2 teaspoons sea salt
50 g (1¾ oz) unsalted butter
80 g (2¾ oz) diced shallot
20 g (¾ oz/ 1½ tablespoons) chopped inner celery stalk
10 fermented black garlic cloves, peeled
750 ml (25½ fl oz/3 cups) Chicken Stock (see Basics, page 240)

Slice the shiitake mushrooms and place in a vacuum-seal bag. Sprinkle over the salt, seal the bag, removing all the air, and leave at room temperature for 24 hours.

The next day, add the butter to a saucepan and sauté the shallots and celery until translucent. Remove the mushrooms from the bag and gently squeeze out any excess liquid, then add the mushrooms to the pan along with the garlic cloves and sauté for 1 minute. Pour over the chicken stock and simmer over a low heat until almost all the liquid has evaporated, then transfer the contents of the pan to a food processor or blender and blitz on high speed for 1 minute. Press the resulting purée through a fine-mesh sieve and refrigerate until needed.

OXTAIL BROTH

2 kg (4 lb 6 oz) oxtail, cut into 5 cm (2 in) rounds
maple chips, for smoking (optional)
100 ml (3½ fl oz) grapeseed oil
100 g (3½ oz) butter
1 brown onion, chopped
2 carrots, chopped
1 celery stalk, chopped
2 garlic cloves
2 bay leaves
10 crushed black peppercorns
3 thyme sprigs
500 ml (17 fl oz/2 cups) oloroso sherry
8 litres (270 fl oz/16 cups) water

If smoking the oxtail, set up a cold smoker with the maple chips. Smoke for 1 hour.

Heat the grapeseed oil and butter in a heavy-based saucepan, add the oxtail, smoked or otherwise, and brown on all sides. Add the vegetables and aromatics to the pan and cook for a further 2–3 minutes, then deglaze with the sherry and reduce until almost all of the liquid has evaporated. Add the water, bring to a simmer and leave to cook over a low heat for 6 hours. Strain the broth, discarding the solids, then bring to the boil and reduce down, skimming off any impurities as you go, until there is only 1 litre (34 fl oz/4 cups) remaining.

UMBRIAN WILD PEAS

300 g (10½ oz) dried Umbrian wild peas,
    soaked in cold water overnight
30 g (1 oz) unsalted butter
30 g (1 oz/2 tablespoons) finely diced shallot
10 g (¼ oz/1 tablespoon) finely diced garlic
750 ml (25½ fl oz/3 cups) Oxtail Broth (see left)

Drain the soaked peas. Melt the butter in a large heavy-based saucepan, add the shallot and garlic and sauté until translucent. Stir in the drained peas, pour over the oxtail broth and simmer over a low heat for 1–1½ hours, or until the peas are just tender to the bite but are still holding their shape.

To serve

Season the braised peas with salt and ground black pepper and top up with the remaining oxtail broth or water if necessary – there should be just enough liquid to serve as a sauce. Reheat the fermented mushroom and black garlic purée. Divide the peas among warmed serving bowls and top each with a spoonful of the purée.

Galeux D'Eysines Pumpkin

FAMILY
CUCURBITACEAE

SPECIES
CUCURBITA MAXIMA

CULTIVAR
GALEUX D'EYSINES

This salmon-coloured pumpkin is a great example of the incredible diversity of heirloom vegetables. Growing up to the 10 kg (22 lb) mark, it is covered in unique peanut shell–like protrusions caused by sugars that leach through the skin as the pumpkin is maturing. The flesh of this pumpkin has an intense orange colour, a beautifully smooth texture and a deep, sweet flavour perfect for slow roasting or turning into a delicious soup. As a bonus, the flowers from this pumpkin are also extremely large and tasty. —— Botanically, Galeux D'Eysines is part of the *Cucurbitaceae* family and belongs to the *Cucurbita maxima* species (pumpkins and squash are generally categorised as either *C. pepo*, *C. maxima* or *C. moschato*). These species are native to Central America and Southwest USA, where they were common wild plants, with remnants of pumpkin seeds having been found in settlements used by indigenous populations in Mexico dating back to 8500 BC. It is believed that by 650 BC pumpkin seeds had spread to China while, following the discovery of the Americas, pumpkins appeared in Europe by the 16th century. Considered a false berry, with the remnants of their calyxes still discernible, pumpkins generally have a thick, angular, rough and somewhat prickly stem. They are the largest of any fruit and take 90–120 days to mature after sowing. —— The Galeux D'Eysines is named after the French town of Eysines where it originated and is mentioned in the French seed producer Vilmorin-Andrieux's famous album, *Des Plantes Potagères*, which dates back to 1883. It has also been referred to as Brode Galeux D'Eysines – while it sounds elegant in French, this translates as 'embroidered with warts from Eysines'.

SLOW-COOKED GALEUX D'EYSINES PUMPKIN, AGED COMTÉ CREAM, TRUFFLE

SERVES 8

This dish takes one of the most humble ingredients and pairs it with one of the most expensive. The combination of the deep, rich flavour of the Galeux D'Eysines pumpkin with the truffle and aged comté is truly indulgent.

SLOW-COOKED PUMPKIN

8 x 5-cm (2-in) thick wedges of Galeux D'Eysines pumpkin (winter squash) or other rich orange-fleshed pumpkin
200 ml (7 fl oz) clarified butter, plus extra if necessary

Place the pumpkin wedges in a large vacuum-seal bag, add the clarified butter and seal, removing all the air. Steam at 95°C (200°F) until the pumpkin feels tender to the touch (approximately 25 minutes). Alternatively, submerge the pumpkin in clarified butter in an ovenproof dish – making sure you have enough butter to cover the pumpkin – and heat in a 95°C (200°F) oven until tender, using a skewer to test the pumpkin for softness. Set aside.

AGED COMTÉ CREAM BASE

20 g (¾ oz/1½ tablespoons) finely diced shallot
5 g (¼ oz/2 teaspoons) finely sliced garlic
20 g (¾ oz) unsalted butter
300 ml (10 fl oz) thickened (whipping) cream

Sauté the shallot and garlic in the butter until translucent.
Add the cream, bring to a vigorous simmer and cook until reduced by one-third. Remove from the heat and set aside until needed.

Additional ingredients

50 g (1¾ oz) crème fraîche
180 g (6½ oz) aged comté, finely grated
1 teaspoon finely grated lemon zest
sea salt
50 g (1¾ oz) fresh black winter truffle, shaved into fine slices
80 ml (2½ fl oz/⅓ cup) Brown Butter (see Basics, page 241), melted

To serve

Preheat the oven to 180°C (350°F) and line a baking tray with non-stick baking paper. Arrange the pumpkin wedges on the prepared tray, transfer to the oven and bake for 7 minutes, or until the pumpkin is hot all the way through.

Meanwhile, bring the comté cream base to a simmer in a medium saucepan, then whisk in the crème fraîche, grated comté and lemon zest and cook for 1–2 minutes until the cheese has melted and the sauce has reduced slightly.

Season the pumpkin wedges with salt to taste and divide among warmed serving plates. Place a generous spoonful of the base sauce next to the pumpkin and layer over the black truffle slices. Brush the truffle slices with the brown butter, sprinkle with sea salt and serve immediately.

Rossa di Verona Chicory

FAMILY
ASTERACEAE

SPECIES
CICHORIUM INTYBUS L.

CULTIVAR
ROSSA DI VERONA SEL. ARCA

Chicories are a diverse group belonging to the *Asteraceae* family. They are generally divided into two types: chicories grown for their taproot – which can be used as a roasted vegetable similar to parsnips or dry roasted and ground and used as a coffee substitute – and those grown for their leaves. ——— Rossa di Verona is a member of the *C. intybus* leaf type, and these chicories are further divided into five main groups: radicchios, sugar loaf, large leaf chicory, catalogna and witloof. Of these groups, the radicchio varieties, including Rossa di Verona, are possibly the best known. Most radicchio varieties have been developed in northern Italy. The Rossa di Verona is a beautiful radicchio with a rounded, solid, compact head, deep red heart-shaped leaves and meaty white stems. ——— Some Italian radicchios, such as Treviso tardiva, are harvested at the end of autumn, trimmed of all their leaves and re-established in a dark warehouse with cold mountain water running over their roots. The new leaves that shoot in these dark conditions develop a bright red colour with large white stems and are more tender and less bitter, making them highly prized and perfect in salads. This process is referred to as forcing, and is similar to that used for Belgian witloof chicory. In a similar manner, I have found that tying a string around the head of Rossa di Verona to close in the outer leaves two weeks before harvesting helps to produce a semi-blanched effect, creating lighter coloured centre leaves that are less bitter and more tender.

CHARRED ROSSA DI VERONA, SHALLOT AND RED WINE VINAIGRETTE

SERVES 8

Radicchios are often treated simply as a bitter leaf salad, or else are roasted or charred. Their aromatic bitterness is considered an aid to digestion and they often accompany a roasted or chargrilled meat.

2 golden shallots
pinch of sea salt
pinch of freshly ground black pepper
75 ml (2½ fl oz) good-quality red-wine vinegar
250 ml (8½ fl oz/1 cup) extra-virgin olive oil
4 Rossa di Verona chicory heads (or other similar radicchio)

Dice the shallots very finely and add them to a bowl together with the salt, pepper and red-wine vinegar. Leave to macerate for 1 hour, then drizzle 150 ml (5 fl oz) of the olive oil into the shallot mixture in a slow stream, whisking as you go, until well emulsified. Set aside.

Cut each head of radicchio in half and wash well under cold water, then pat dry and coat in the remaining 100 ml (3½ fl oz) olive oil. Set two large, heavy-based frying pans over a high heat and, once hot, add the radicchio halves, cut side down. Cook until nicely coloured – about 1 minute on each side – then transfer to a serving platter and dress liberally with the vinaigrette. Serve.

'Little Pink' Potato

FAMILY
SOLANACEAE

SPECIES
SOLANUM TUBEROSUM

CULTIVAR
LITTLE PINK

Potatoes are one of the world's most important food crops, behind only maize, wheat and rice in terms of scale of production. The potato is believed to have first been domesticated between 8000–5000 BC in the region comprising modern-day southern Peru and the extreme northwest of Bolivia. —— Introduced into Europe in the second half of the 16th century by the Spanish, potatoes were initially received with scepticism by European farmers. To encourage the French to accept the potato, for example, pharmacist Antoine-Augustin Parmentier coined the term *pomme de terre* ('apple of the earth') and it is said that he was so determined for their introduction to be a success that he persuaded Marie Antoinette to wear the delicate white flowers of the potato plant in her hair at court. Potatoes eventually became a widely planted crop in Europe due to their high yield per acre (the potato has the greatest yield of calories per acre at about 9.2 million compared with wheat at three million), with conservative estimates showing that their introduction to the continent was directly responsible for one-quarter of the growth in European population and urbanisation over the period 1700–1900. However, due to the lack of genetic diversity in these potatoes first introduced to Europe, they eventually became susceptible to disease. During the summer of 1845, spores of the fungus *Phytopthora infestans* were windblown across the Channel to England from France, where they wreaked havoc among English potatoes. Ireland, where the potato had been welcomed as a godsend as the plant grew well in the country's moist and relatively frost-free climate, was infected that September with devastating results – most potato crops were lost in 1845 and all were lost in 1846. Subsequently, starvation and disease stalked the land, with over one million people losing their lives: a catastrophe that also resulted in a further two and a half million people leaving the country on immigration ships in search of a better life. ——There are estimated to be more than 5000 varieties of potatoes worldwide with the vast majority found in the Andes, where more than 100 cultivars might be found in a single valley and a dozen or so might be maintained by a single agricultural household. —— The potatoes featured here were gifted to me by a Peruvian chef. He was unaware of the name of these potatoes and the closest translation he could come up with was 'little pinks'. This is not surprising – as I have mentioned there are literally thousands of varieties of potatoes available and an even greater variety of common names to describe them. Another variety of pink-fleshed potato that is available in Australia are Cranberry Reds, although these produce a larger potato; my little pinks are more closely related to the fingerling varieties, which are generally small and waxy. (For the recipe overleaf you could experiment with many types of small potato – another one of my favourite varieties that would work well is the Jersey Royal.) —— Nothing quite compares to digging up home-grown potatoes and consuming them within a couple of hours; at this point their sugars haven't all converted to starch and they are naturally sweet and especially delicious.

STEAMED 'LITTLE PINK' POTATOES
WITH POTATO EMULSION AND CAVIAR

There are many interesting varieties of potatoes available, with flesh colours ranging from deep gold to beetroot red through to purple. These 'little pink' potatoes are delicious, with a dense, waxy flesh that absorbs rich flavours well. Here, these humble potatoes are paired with one of the most luxurious, intensely flavoured ingredients – caviar.

NOTE: *This recipe calls for a whipping syphon (cream whipper) to aerate the potato mixture, though it isn't essential – it will just be a little denser in texture without.*

300 g (10½ oz) Dutch Cream potatoes or other waxy potato variety
300 ml (10 fl oz) thickened (whipping) cream
sea salt
1.2 kg (2 lb 10 oz) 'little pink' waxy potatoes or
other pink-fleshed potato variety such as Cranberry Red
100 ml (3½ fl oz) melted butter
30 g (1 oz/2½ tablespoons) ossetra caviar

Add the Dutch Cream potatoes to a steamer basket set over simmering water and steam until tender. Peel off the skins and pass the potatoes through a potato ricer. Weigh out 200 g (7 oz) of the riced potato flesh, transfer it to a small saucepan and cover with a lid.

Bring the cream to the boil in a separate saucepan, then remove from the heat, whisk in the warm riced potato flesh and season to taste with sea salt. Transfer the mixture to a charged whipping syphon (cream whipper) and shake well. (Alternatively, simply spoon this mixture into a bowl.) Set aside at room temperature.

Steam the little pink potatoes until tender, then carefully remove the skins with a paring knife. Briefly re-steam the potatoes until hot, then transfer to a bowl, brush with the melted butter and season with sea salt. Squeeze some potato emulsion from the whipping syphon onto each warmed serving bowl. Arrange a small pile of little pinks over the emulsion, place a teaspoon of caviar on top of each mound, along with more potato emulsion, if you like. Serve immediately.

Shimonita Onion (One-year Onion)

FAMILY
AMARYLLIDACEAE

SPECIES
ALLIUM FISTULOSUM

CULTIVAR
SHIMONITA NEGI

Famed for its fat white root ends and wonderful sweet flavour when cooked, the shimonita onion is a unique Japanese bunching onion that forms a single stalk only. Originating from the town of Shimonita in Japan, it is referred to as the 'King of the *negi*' (the Japanese term for all bunching green onions), though in appearance it looks more like a leek than a typical bunching onion. —— Shimonita onions are traditionally planted in autumn and harvested at the same time the following year (hence their alternate common name, the 'one-year onion'). While they can be harvested and eaten as younger, thinner spring green onions, to fully appreciate their unique characteristics you should let them mature and form their large swollen white stalks. These are strong when eaten raw and are best cooked – either slowly, which renders them meltingly soft and deliciously sweet, or cut into pieces and briefly charcoal-grilled. —— Shimonita onions are hardy and require just a warm sunny position with good, composted soil and a reasonable amount of watering. I have found them to be very easy to grow, though when I first did so in Australia I noticed that our much milder winters led to them being fully mature by early summer, meaning that I didn't need to wait until autumn to harvest (making them three quarter–year onions). Since then I have planted them in early spring and harvested them fully grown in autumn. Shimonita is a very sculptural vegetable to have in your garden; while the onions' large hollow green tops are impressive enough, when they start to form their large white spherical flower heads – which open up like giant pompoms – they go to the next level (though bear in mind that you should only allow this if you intend to keep the seed, harvesting the onions prior to flowering to prevent them from diverting all their energy towards this goal).

SHIMONITA ONIONS, SQUID, GARLIC CREAM, GREEN ALMONDS

SERVES 8

Sautéing shimonita onions in butter renders them soft and sweet. Here, I have set them off with the textural counterpoints of thinly sliced squid and crisp, new season's green almonds, rounding out the dish with a garlic cream that brings everything together.

220 g (8 oz) unsalted butter
3 garlic cloves, peeled
500 ml (17 fl oz/2 cups) milk
5 g (¼ oz/1 teaspoon) agar agar powder
sea salt
2 large or 4 small shimonita onions
2 x 150 g (5½ oz) squid tubes, cleaned
about 40 green almonds (or regular blanched almonds), shelled, peeled and halved
about 40 white Society Garlic flowers or chive flowers

For the garlic cream, melt 20 g (¾ oz) of the butter in a heavy-based saucepan, add the garlic cloves and sauté over a medium heat until softened but not coloured. Add the milk and bring it close to boiling point, then remove the pan from the heat and leave the garlic to infuse in the milk for 20 minutes.

Pour the infused milk through a fine-mesh sieve into a clean saucepan and discard the solids. Set the pan over a medium heat, whisk in the agar agar and continue to heat, whisking, until the milk reaches 90°C (195°F). Season with sea salt to taste, then transfer to a suitable container and refrigerate until set. Once set, transfer the garlic cream to a blender and blitz on high speed to form a smooth paste. Refrigerate until needed (it will keep for up to 5 days).

Strip the outer leaves off the shimonita onions and discard along with the green tops. Cut the white stalks into 3 cm (1¼ in) thick discs.

Place one of the squid tubes on a chopping board, cut along one side with a sharp knife and open the tube out like a book, then trim the edges and cut 2 mm (⅛ in) thick strips from the width of the body. Repeat with the remaining squid tube.

Melt 100 g (3½ oz) of the remaining unsalted butter in a large non-stick frying pan over a high heat, add the sliced onions and sauté, stirring occasionally, for 2 minutes, or until the onions are wilted and beginning to soften. Remove the onions from the pan, drain off any excess liquid and season with sea salt. Keep warm.

Wipe the frying pan clean and return to the heat with the remaining 100 g (3½ oz) of butter. Once the butter has melted, add the sliced squid and sauté briefly (as soon as the squid turns opaque it is ready), then add the green almonds, season with sea salt and stir to combine. Remove the mixture from the pan and drain off any excess liquid.

Meanwhile, warm 150 ml (5 fl oz) of the garlic cream in a small saucepan until it reaches a mayonnaise-like consistency.

To serve, place a few spoonfuls of the sautéed onions in the centre of each serving plate. Top the onions with the squid and almonds, dot with the garlic cream and scatter over the garlic flowers to finish.

TIM AND LIZ JOHNSTONE

JOHNSTONE'S KITCHEN GARDENS

Tim Johnstone is one of my main suppliers of heirloom vegetables, herbs and edible
flowers, and I have been working closely with him and his wife, Liz, since 2011.
Tim first contacted me after he read an article in the *Organic Gardener Magazine*
about my test garden and passion for heirloom and rare vegetables, and how I was
working with small independent growers to produce vegetables for Quay Restaurant.
Tim asked what he could grow for me and this became the beginning of a very fruitful
relationship that has continued to this day.

In his own words, Tim describes how he got started in agriculture and
a little about his philosophy and passion for growing –

I grew up hearing stories about my family's history and how my ancestors had been active
in various agricultural pursuits. Many generations ago my family had an orchard and a
chicken farm in Ryde (the land of the Granny Smith apple) in what is now a residential suburb
of Sydney. My parents fondly tell stories about my bank clerk grandfather spending pretty
much all of his spare time growing veggies for family and friends. My dad was a career
schoolteacher and always had a large veggie plot and small orchard when I was growing up,
and a large chunk of my childhood years were spent on the family smallholding in the foothills
of the Blue Mountains. While not always an active participant (child labour), I was always
drawn to observing how things worked and related to one another – something that made a
lot of sense to me when I studied agro-ecosystems as part of my agriculture degree in my
early twenties.

My older brother Mark had a passion for growing too, and was a significant influence
in our farming journey. Without his help we may never have gotten off the ground as an
operational farm. Although he passed away suddenly in mid-2013, I have some amazing
memories of working with him – both of us with our hands in the ground doing something we
loved. There are also the funny memories of when equipment broke and we would each blame
the other, as it couldn't have been our fault!

When our kids were very small we basically turned a small rental on a 550 m (1,800 ft)
block in Western Sydney into a productive permaculture paradise, then, when the opportunity
came up in 2010 to rent a 4 acre block nearby, we jumped at it. Over the eight years we have
been growing commercially we have ploughed pretty much every cent into building a small
business doing what we love – growing veggies, herbs, garnishes and edible flowers. We have
grown from operating a quarter-acre garden with no infrastructure to approximately 6 acres,
1 to 2 acres of which is polytunnels and all the equipment, tools and machinery needed to
make it work. When we were at our largest we worked out that our little farm was helping
to feed approximately 150–200 families, supplying about twenty restaurants and directly
contributing to supporting seven families. Not a bad feat on a small parcel of land.

We are firm believers that all farmers – no matter what their ideology or the farming principles they follow – work very hard and are, at their core, stewards of the land. Some farming practices have more direct impacts on our immediate world (our soil) and the wider planet. Due to our previous experience in conventional agriculture we made a very conscious decision early on to grow organically. I figured if it was good enough for my grandfather and great grandfather – who didn't have access to the synthetics we do today – then it was good enough for us. Especially when you consider that whatever you put onto your plants and gardens will be a part of you shortly!

What does it mean to me to grow organically in today's world? We work in tune with nature as much as we can with the tools we have available in the 21st century. Organic gardening generally requires a lot of labour, but there is nothing so powerful as taking a tiny seed and growing something to feed yourself, your family and your friends.

Two critical factors to successfully grow plants are healthy, robust soil and available moisture. It might not seem like rocket science, but it can take a lot of work and working out to make this happen day in, day out in a changing world. Get your soil and moisture levels right and you have the right conditions to grow a plant. To help it achieve its optimal growth there are many, many variables.

Ninety-five per cent of the varieties we grow are open-pollinated. Part of the reason is that the diverse genetic variability can help adapt to prevailing conditions. In the case of peas, we have seed saved for over five generations as a key way for us to be able to select from a local population for both good production and greater tolerance to disease.

Growing is challenging and rewarding, as are relationships. The long-term relationship we have with Peter is an amazing balance of pushing the boundaries of what we can do on the farm as well as what can be done in the kitchen. While we don't always see eye to eye on varieties, costings and the feasibility of some lines, the benefit to both of us is that from this challenge a fantastic product is produced.

Peter makes regular visits to the farm to discuss how things are going and to plan upcoming lines, and a real joy for both of us is going through seed catalogues and testing out 'new' or 'old' varieties to see what they can do across their whole lifecycle. Peter might not want the leaf, fruit or bulb; it might be the root, flower or seed. This means we are constantly pushing and trying new things – both in the garden and on the plate. These visits are always an exciting time, and we generally get out the seed packets and catalogues and look for interesting things to try. These collaborative meetings are a great opportunity to discuss the potential for new and innovative veggies and to strengthen the connection between the Quay kitchen and the farm – one that is enhanced by our twice-weekly deliveries to the restaurant.

Ice Plant

FAMILY
AIZOACEAE

SPECIES
MESEMBRANTHEMUM CRYSTALLINUM

CULTIVAR
SALTY ICE PLANT

I ce plant is a succulent herb from the *Aizoaceae* family, a group containing a number of unusual plants that look like pebbles or stones (often called stone plants). Though native to southern and western Africa, the ice plant has been naturalised in Australia – a result of the leaves having historically been used to treat scurvy on long voyages, which has led to its occurrence worldwide – and is related to native greens such as saltbush, sea blite and Warrigal greens. —— Ice plant's ability to take up salt has seen it spread through coastal regions of southern and western Australia. Interestingly, when the plant dies it releases salt back into the surrounding soil, dehydrating it and preventing the growth of other plants. The seeds of the salty ice plant, however, can germinate in this environment and so the plant can self-propagate with ease. As a result, it has even become invasive in some coastal areas. —— Ice plants have lots of large bladder cells, which give them their distinctive glistening appearance, like ice crystals. Salty Ice Plant is a special cultivar – its leaves and flower buds are edible and have a distinct, salty flavour. Being succulent and crispy, they make an excellent addition to salads.

SALAD OF SALTY ICE PLANT, WHOLE LEMON CREAM, BROAD BEANS, NASTURTIUMS AND PEPITAS

SERVES 8

In this salad, crunchy ice plant is played off against lush whole lemon cream. The lemon flavour works well with the salty, iodine tang of the ice plant, while the supporting ingredients of young broad beans and crunchy pepitas lend the dish good textural contrast.

4 lemons
1–2 tablespoons water
250 g (9 oz/1 cup) crème fraîche
70–80 blanched and double-shelled broad (fava) beans
2 tablespoons lightly roasted pepitas (pumpkin seeds)
about 20 small dark-green nasturtium leaves
100 ml (3½ fl oz) extra-virgin olive oil
pinch of sea salt
32 Salty Ice Plant sprigs

Bring a large saucepan of water to the boil, add the lemons and boil for 2 minutes. Drain the lemons, then re-fill the saucepan with water and repeat the process a further three times – this will cook and soften the lemons and extract some of their harsher, bitter flavours.

After the fourth blanching, cut the lemons into quarters and, using a sharp knife, remove the flesh and seeds, leaving behind the thick pith and peel. Discard the flesh and seeds, transfer the lemon rinds to a food processor and blitz on a high speed to form a purée, adding 1–2 tablespoons of water to thin it out a little if necessary. Pass the purée through a fine-mesh sieve and set aside to cool.

Once cool, measure out 150 g (5½ oz) of the sieved lemon purée into a bowl, add the crème fraîche and whisk together until incorporated. Place in the refrigerator until needed.

When ready to serve, toss the broad beans, pepitas and nasturtium leaves together with the olive oil and sea salt in a small bowl. Spoon three or four teaspoons of lemon cream onto individual serving plates and top each with four ice plant sprigs. Scatter over the dressed broad beans, pepitas and nasturtium leaves and serve.

Trentino Cabbage Turnip

FAMILY
BRASSICACEAE

SPECIES
BRASSICA OLERACEA

CULTIVAR
NAONE ROSSE ANTICA TRENTINO

I first came across the Trentino cabbage turnip in an article by Joseph Simcox of The Rare Vegetable Seed Consortium. A self-described 'botanical explorer', Joe travels the world in search of rare and unusual fruits and vegetables, collecting and saving seeds, and discovered this particular vegetable at a rare vegetable seed exchange in Northern Italy. According to Plinio Pancirolle, the editor of the regional country association for the northern Italian region of Trentino, the Naone Rosse Antica has been raised in the area for more than 2000 continuous years, a claim substantiated by historical records. —— Despite the name, Plinio and his colleagues claim that the Trentino cabbage turnip, because of its flavour, texture and leaves, is not actually part of the *brassica rapa* (turnip) species, but belongs to *brassica oleracea* (cabbage) instead. Botanical information in this area shows extensive crossover between brassica species with many overlapping and conflicting definitions – whichever way it goes, this is a unique and ancient vegetable that needs to be celebrated. It has a succulent texture and mild flavour that is best enjoyed raw. ——When I first grew this vegetable, I planted the seeds in mid-autumn. It did take some time for the swollen taproot to develop, but it became very large by early spring – about the size of a soccer ball. There are two varieties of the Trentino cabbage turnip available, the red-skinned, red-leafed variety Naone Rosse Antica, and the green-skinned variety Naone Giallo Antica. Both varieties have white flesh and are equally delicious.

SALAD OF RAW TRENTINO CABBAGE TURNIP WITH CAPER VINAIGRETTE

SERVES 8

Like a cross between celeriac and kohlrabi, the flavour of this rare cabbage turnip lends itself well to this caper vinaigrette preparation. This salad would make a great accompaniment to roast chicken.

1 large Trentino cabbage turnip
2 tablespoons salted capers, rinsed
1 tablespoon finely diced shallot
½ teaspoon finely diced garlic
2 tablespoons lemon juice
70 ml (2¼ fl oz) good-quality apple-cider vinegar
sea salt and freshly ground black pepper
200 ml (7 fl oz) extra-virgin olive oil
1 tablespoon finely julienned flat-leaf (Italian) parsley
1 tablespoon sliced chives
about 30 pea tendrils
about 30 pea flowers
about 40 small nasturtium leaves

Use a sharp knife to peel the cabbage turnip, then cut it into thin 1 cm (½-in) wide ribbons using a mandoline. Transfer the ribbons to a large bowl of iced water and leave for 1 hour.

Meanwhile, add the capers, shallot, garlic, lemon juice, vinegar and a pinch each of salt and pepper to a bowl and mix well. Leave to macerate for 1 hour.

Once macerated, slowly whisk the extra-virgin olive oil into the caper mixture to form an emulsion, then stir through the parsley and chives.

Drain and dry the cabbage turnip ribbons well, add to the bowl with the vinaigrette and toss together. Place the dressed cabbage turnip on a large platter and garnish with the pea tendrils, pea flowers and nasturtium leaves.

Scorzonera (Black Salsify)

FAMILY
ASTERACEAE

SPECIES
SCORZONERA HISPANICA

CULTIVAR
DUPLEX

S corzonera, or black salsify as it is also known, is a member of the *Asteraceae* daisy family that includes lettuce, Jerusalem artichoke, dandelion and white salsify. Cultivated for its long, edible taproots, which grow up to 50 cm (20 in) in length, it is believed to have originated in southern Europe and the Near East and is generally thought to have spread from Spain to the rest of Europe. Also known as serpent root, viper's grass and oyster plant, it has been claimed that the name 'scorzonera' is derived from the old French word *scorzone*, meaning snake or adder, though it is more likely to come from the Italian *scorza negra*, meaning black bark. —— Typical of the daisy family, the scorzonera roots produce a milky white sap that quickly discolours the flesh, so it must be immersed in acidulated water (water with lemon juice or vinegar) immediately after peeling to avoid discolouration. The roots generally need about twenty minutes on a gentle simmer to become tender and their flavour, once cooked, is earthy and nutty – akin to asparagus and artichoke – though some people perceive an oyster-like flavour as well. Scorzonera has a very high vitamin E content, which acts as an antioxidant, as well as being high in vitamin B1 and magnesium, which are said to support the nervous system. —— Although scorzonera was cultivated as a vegetable in Italy and France as early as 1660 – with the Belgians growing vast fields of it soon thereafter – it is no longer widely grown and is now the reserve of small-scale market gardeners, though it has become popular with chefs as a result of its unique flavour and interesting texture. It is generally harvested in late autumn, when the flavour is at its peak, and stores well over winter, though it can be difficult to harvest as the roots are quite fragile and can lose their freshness when broken.

SCORZONERA, ROASTED CHICKEN SKIN, CONFIT EGG YOLK

SERVES 8

Scorzonera is a lovely root vegetable with a nutty, earthy flavour. Here, it is coated with sesame seeds, pan fried and served with roasted chicken skin, confit egg yolk and a little aïoli.

ROASTED CHICKEN SKIN

250 g (9 oz) fresh chicken skin
olive oil
sea salt

Preheat the oven to 180°C (350°F) and line a heavy-based baking tray with baking paper. Place the chicken skin on a chopping board, underside up, and scrape away as much fat as possible using a sharp knife. Brush the skin with a little olive oil and sprinkle with sea salt, then spread it out over the prepared baking tray, ensuring it is completely flat. Cover the skin with another sheet of baking paper, then place another heavy-based baking tray on top to sandwich it in place. Place in the oven and roast for 12–15 minutes, or until the skin is golden brown, then transfer the skin to a wire rack to cool. Break into small pieces and set aside until needed.

SCORZONERA

1 litre (34 fl oz/4 cups) water
juice of 1¼ lemons
16 scorzonera roots
2 garlic cloves, finely sliced
2 thyme sprigs
400 ml (13½ fl oz) olive oil
plain (all-purpose) flour, for coating
2 eggs, beaten
100 g (3½ oz/⅔ cup) white sesame seeds
100 g (3½ oz/4 cups) puffed amaranth

Combine the water with the juice of one lemon in a bowl. Using a vegetable peeler, peel a scorzonera root and plunge it straight into the acidulated water to avoid it discolouring, then repeat with the remaining roots.

Once all the roots are peeled, remove the scorzonera from the water and cut into 8 cm (3¼ in) lengths, then add to a vacuum-seal bag together with the garlic, thyme, remaining lemon juice and 300 ml (10½ fl oz) of the olive oil. Seal the bag, removing all the air, and steam at 95°C (200°F) for approximately 20 minutes, or until tender. Alternatively, add the scorzonera and oil mixture to a baking tray and cook in a 180°C (350°F) oven for 30 minutes. Drain and pat dry with paper towel.

Place the flour, beaten egg, sesame seeds and puffed amaranth in separate shallow bowls. Lightly flour the scorzonera pieces, coat with the egg and then roll in the sesame seeds and puffed amaranth.

Heat the remaining 100 ml (3½ fl oz) olive oil in a non-stick frying pan over a medium–high heat. Working in batches, add the scorzonera pieces to the pan and fry until golden brown on all sides. Drain on paper towel and keep warm in a low oven.

CONFIT EGG YOLK

250 ml (8½ fl oz/1 cup) Brown Butter (see Basics, page 241), melted
8 egg yolks

Divide the brown butter among eight plastic dariole moulds and carefully place an unbroken egg yolk in each. Cover each mould tightly with plastic wrap and place in a 65°C (150°F) steamer for approximately 10 minutes, or until the yolks are just set.

Additional ingredients

zest of ½ lemon
125 ml (4 fl oz/½ cup) Aïoli (see Basics, page 241)
60 winter purslane sprigs

To serve

Mix the lemon zest together with the aïoli. Set aside.

Add a spoonful of aïoli to the centre of each of eight warmed serving plates. Surround the aïoli with pieces of scorzonera and chicken skin and scatter over the winter purslane. Carefully remove the warmed egg yolks from the dariole moulds with a slotted spoon and lower onto the aïoli. Serve immediately.

Tatume Squash

FAMILY
CUCURBITACEAE

SPECIES
CUCURBITA PEPO

CULTIVAR
TATUME

The Tatume squash is an heirloom, open-pollinated summer squash and a staple of Mexican cooking. A member of the *Cucurbitaceae* family – which also includes pumpkins, zucchinis, cucumbers, melons and gourds – it falls into one of three species of summer and winter squash, *Cucurbita pepo* (the other two being *C. maxima* and *C. moschate*). The word 'squash' is derived from the Narragansett Native American word *askutasquash*, which means 'eaten raw'. Botanists believe this species to have originated primarily as wild plants in Mesoamerica, home to the Incas, Mayans and Aztecs, while archaeological evidence shows that gardeners in the region have been growing different varieties of *C. pepo* for more than 8000 years, predating the domestication of corn. *C. pepo* spread to China in early history, where remnants dating back to 650 BC have been found. ——— The fruit of the Tatume squash are elongated in shape with striped green skin resembling a small growing watermelon. They are best harvested young, when half the size of a football, at which point the fresh seeds are delicious raw. The flesh can be either briefly sautéed as you would a zucchini, or gently cooked in a braise. ——— The Tatume squash is easy to grow, and prolific – with beautiful sprawling vines, large green, silvery leaves and yellow trumpet-like flowers – though, as each node on a vine can root and send out other vines, if you plan on growing it you should make sure you have plenty of room. It is ideally grown in summer and requires full sun and well-drained, loamy soil (like other curcubits it is best planted in mounds to avoid 'wet feet') with a mid-range pH for good growth. Bees are attracted to the squash's large flowers, making pollination straightforward, while the excess male flowers can be eaten as you would zucchini flowers and are delicious. ——— To me, the flavour of Tatume squash is far superior to the average zucchini, though in my experience of growing it I have found the squash can grow from the size of a cherry to that of a football within a week. If you want to catch it at a good young stage, when the flesh and skin are very tender and the seeds soft, you will need to keep a close eye on your patch.

TATUME SQUASH, LIME BEURRE BLANC, NEW SEASON'S MACADAMIA NUTS

SERVES 8

The flavour of a freshly picked young Tatume squash is delicately sweet. So as not to overpower its subtlety,
I like to keep its preparation simple – in this recipe the squash is paired with a classic beurre blanc with the addition
of lime, while young green macadamia nuts make for a serendipitous seasonal and textural companion.

LIME BEURRE BLANC

250 g (9 oz) unsalted butter, diced and chilled
1 shallot, finely diced
½ garlic clove, finely diced
juice of ½ lime

Melt 40 g (1½ oz) of the butter in a saucepan over a medium heat,
add the shallot and garlic and gently sauté until translucent. Add
half the lime juice, then whisk in the remaining butter a few pieces
at a time until all the butter is incorporated and your sauce is thick
and glossy. Strain the beurre blanc through a fine-mesh sieve and
return to the pan, discarding the shallots and garlic. Season to
taste, add the remaining lime juice and keep warm.

Additional ingredients

100 g (3½ oz) unsalted butter
1 baseball-sized Tatume squash, peeled and cut into 8 wedges
sea salt
zest of 1 lime
1 bunch fresh elderflower heads, blossoms picked
about 20 fresh new season's macadamia nuts, shelled and halved
   (or regular macadamia nuts)
about 30 young purslane sprigs

To serve

Melt the butter in a large non-stick frying pan over a medium heat,
add the squash pieces and cook for about 1 minute on each side
until tender and only slightly coloured (lower the heat if the squash
are colouring too quickly). Remove the squash pieces from the pan,
drain off any excess butter and season with sea salt, then divide
evenly among warmed serving plates.

   Stir the lime zest through the beurre blanc. Spoon the warm
sauce over the squash pieces, sprinkle over the elderflower
blossoms and scatter over the macadamia nuts and purslane
sprigs to finish. Serve.

White Asparagus

FAMILY
ASPARAGACEAE

SPECIES
ASPARAGUS OFFICINALIS

CULTIVAR
PRECOCE D'ARGENTEUIL

O ften referred to as a 'noble' or 'royal' plant, asparagus is considered by many to be the king of vegetables. It is grown for its tender edible shoots, which are usually green when exposed to sunlight (though there are also some purple-skinned varieties) or white when deprived of light through a process called 'blanching', whereby soil is mounded over the growing beds as soon as the shoots emerge. Both growing methods produce a delicious vegetable, but it is the white asparagus that is most highly prized for its tenderness and delicate flavour. —— *Asparagus officinalis* is thought to have originated in the Caucasian and Siberian regions of eastern Europe, where it is also believed to have been domesticated. The Ancient Greeks and Romans took the practice of growing asparagus from these eastern areas along with the old Iranian word *sparega* (meaning shoot, rod or spray) becoming *aspárago's* and *asparagus* in Greek and Latin respectively. However, although the Romans spread the culture of growing asparagus throughout western Europe, the decline of the Roman empire also saw the decline of European asparagus cultivation, and it wasn't until the Renaissance that asparagus was rediscovered and became popular again for eating. —— The rhizome (crown) is the perennial part of the asparagus plant and is composed of clusters of buds. In spring these buds sprout tender shoots (spears) growing up to 25 cm (10 in) in length. It is these spears that are harvested as a vegetable, though if the spears continue to grow they will form fern-like branches, which will eventually flower, fruit and seed (the small red berries that contain the seeds should not be eaten as they are poisonous). —— Asparagus grows best in coarse, sandy, loamy soils and requires good amounts of organic matter, though it can also grow in richer soils if they are well drained. Asparagus can either be grown from seed or from one-year-old crowns. It is best not to harvest the spears for the first two years, as the ferns are needed to generate energy to establish strong crowns. Once established, crowns can last and be productive for up to fifteen years. —— There are hundreds of different asparagus cultivars available, with selective breeding responsible for the largest, fattest asparagus spears. Precoce D'Argenteuil is a widely available cultivar developed in France in 1830 specifically for the production of white asparagus. It has a delicate flavour and produces large, tender spears with tips that are lightly coloured with a pink to purple hue.

WHITE ASPARAGUS RISOTTO

SERVES 8

White asparagus is such a luxurious vegetable. I often just boil the spears and enjoy them with a traditional hollandaise or melted butter, though they are also delicious shaved raw in a salad, or made into a risotto like this.

The very best white asparagus available in Australia is grown in Tasmania by a man called Richard Weston, who is, I believe, the only person in the country to grow the true European white asparagus varieties. In this recipe I have enhanced the asparagus flavour by using the trimmings to produce a dehydrated powder, while the asparagus itself is cut into both julienne and larger pieces to provide a change of texture within the dish.

24 large Precoce D'Argenteuil white asparagus spears (or other white asparagus spears),
woody ends removed and discarded
2 litres (68 fl oz/8 cups) Chicken Stock or Vegetable Stock (see Basics, page 240)
100 g (3½ oz) unsalted butter
2 shallots, finely diced
½ garlic clove, finely diced
300 g (10½ oz) arborio rice
100 g (3½ oz) parmesan, finely grated
sea salt
2 tablespoons toasted white sesame seeds
50 ml (1¾ fl oz) extra-virgin olive oil

Slice the heads off the asparagus spears and set aside. Peel the remaining stalks with a vegetable peeler, then transfer ten of the peeled stalks to a wire rack and dehydrate in a dehydrator or a very low oven preheated to 50°C (120°F) for 12 hours, or until the asparagus can snap and is completely dry. Place in a spice grinder and grind to a powder. Weigh out 20 g (¾ oz) and set aside in an airtight container until needed.

Slice half of the remaining asparagus stalks into 2 mm (⅛ in) thick pieces on the diagonal and cut the rest into julienne. Set two saucepans on the stove top, filling one with the stock and the other with salted water. Bring both to the boil.

Melt 50 g (1¾ oz) of the unsalted butter in another saucepan over a medium–high heat, add the shallots and garlic and gently sauté until translucent. Add the rice and stir to coat well, then start adding the stock a ladleful at a time, stirring every minute or so and adding the next ladleful only once the rice has absorbed the liquid, for approximately 15 minutes, or until the rice is al dente; at this point you should have just a little stock left. Add the sliced asparagus and stir for another minute, then stir in the remaining butter and 80 g (2¾ oz) of the parmesan. Season to taste with salt and add a little more stock at this point if the risotto looks like it needs it, then turn off the heat and leave to sit for 2 minutes.

While the risotto is sitting, add the asparagus heads to the saucepan of boiling salted water and blanch for 1 minute. Remove from the pan with a slotted spoon and drain on a clean tea towel (dish towel). Add the julienned asparagus stalks to the pan and blanch for 30 seconds. Drain.

Combine the asparagus powder with the sesame seeds and remaining parmesan.

Divide the risotto among serving plates and scatter over the blanched asparagus heads and julienned stalks. Drizzle over the extra-virgin olive oil and sprinkle over a generous amount of the asparagus powder and sesame seed mixture. Serve.

PETER GILMORE

Cherokee White Eagle Corn

FAMILY
POACEAE

SPECIES
ZEA MAYS

CULTIVAR
CHEROKEE WHITE EAGLE

Cherokee White Eagle corn is a beautiful traditional heirloom that has been grown by the Cherokee – skilled farmers and stewards of many traditional varieties of corn, beans and squash – in their native home of the south-eastern United States for hundreds of years. It travelled with the Cherokee during their forced relocation to Oklahoma in the 1830s, a journey now referred to as 'the trail of tears'. The corn's kernels come in varying striking shades of purple and white, with some having an indent and others markings that resemble the outline of an eagle (an important symbol for the Cherokee), hence the name. —— Historically, the Cherokee grew White Eagle corn (and indeed all their corn) following the 'Three Sisters' technique: a style of companion planting that was practised by many ancient indigenous Mesoamerican cultures and dates back at least 6000 years. Following this system, corn, beans and squash are planted close together in a staggered fashion, with the three crops benefitting each other – the corn providing the structure for the beans to climb, the beans providing the nitrogen for the soil that the other plants use, and the squash spreading along the ground to block the sunlight, help prevent the establishment of weeds and act as a living mulch, creating a microclimate to retain moisture levels in the soil. This system was used to produce food that would store well so the heirlooms that were developed over the centuries were chosen for their storage attributes, with everything harvested at a mature stage – in this way these ancient cultures could ensure their survival through long, lean winters. —— I was gifted some White Eagle corn by Stephen Smith, who runs Sacred Eagle Seedhouse in Guthrie, Kentucky and has one of the largest collections of heirloom corn in the world. I first met Stephen at the National Heirloom Expo in California, where he was exhibiting some of his rare heirloom corns (he has also written a couple of books on the subject) that come from all over the Americas, Peru, Mexico and the southern United States. When I grew White Eagle in my garden I was super impressed with the vigour of the plants – the germination rate was very high, the corn developed quickly and most stalks formed at least two ears. At their young, tender 'milk' stage (the point at which the milky sap comes out of the kernels easily), the cobs can be roasted and enjoyed fresh; allowed to fully mature and dry, the corn makes an excellent ground flour or a more coarsely ground cornmeal with a beautiful purple hue.

WHITE EAGLE CORN CRUMPETS, OCEAN TROUT CAVIAR

I have used Cherokee White Eagle corn in the form of cornmeal to make these crumpets. You could just grind the dry corn into meal and proceed with the recipe but, in this case, I have experimented with sprouting the dried corn to release more of the nutrients it contains, which also has the effect of improving the texture of the cornmeal and makes it more easily digestible. After sprouting the corn, it needs to be dehydrated again to be able to be ground. I have found that this process makes an interesting alternative to the nixtamalization process traditionally used in Mexico, as it results in a similar texture but a more natural corn taste.

200 g (7 oz) dried Cherokee White Eagle corn kernels
400 ml (13½ fl oz) milk
1 tablespoon caster (superfine) sugar
10 g (¼ oz/1 teaspoon) dried yeast
100 g (3½ oz) plain (all-purpose) flour
1 teaspoon bicarbonate of soda (baking soda)
2 tablespoons melted butter
½ teaspoon sea salt
approx. 100 ml (3½ fl oz) clarified butter
100 g (3½ oz) unsalted cultured butter, softened
250 g (9 oz) ocean trout caviar

If you choose to sprout the corn before grinding, place the dried kernels in a large bowl, cover with filtered water and leave to soak for 1 hour, then remove from the water and place in a sprouting jar or spread out on a damp, clean muslin (cheesecloth). Follow the directions for sprouting if using a sprouting jar or, alternatively, cover the corn with another layer of damp muslin. The corn will take 3–4 days to sprout – if using the muslin method, re-dampen the muslin cloth with a little water every 12 hours. At the first sign of the corn sprouting, stop the sprouting process by laying the corn out on a baking tray lined with dry silicone paper. Dehydrate the corn in a low 50–60°C (120–140°F) dehydrator or oven until the corn is completely dry, approximately 8 hours.

To grind the corn, place the dried kernels (sprouted or otherwise) in a coffee grinder and whizz to a fine powder, then pass through a fine-mesh sieve to remove any rough, large pieces and measure out 150 g (5½ oz). Set aside until needed (it will keep in an airtight container in the refrigerator for 2–3 months).

When ready to cook, gently warm 100 ml (3½ fl oz) of the milk in a heavy-based saucepan together with the caster sugar. Add the dried yeast and stir well to dissolve, then transfer to a large bowl and set aside in a warm place for 1 hour to allow the yeast to activate.

Combine the measured cornmeal, flour and bicarbonate of soda in a separate clean bowl.

Warm the remaining 300 ml (10 fl oz) of milk in a saucepan over a very gentle heat to no more than 35°C (95°F). Stir in the melted butter, then pour the contents of the pan over the milk and yeast mixture and stir together well. Add the combined dry ingredients to the bowl and stir well to form a batter. Cover the bowl with plastic wrap and leave in a warm place for 1 hour, then gently stir through the sea salt.

Brush eight 10 x 3 cm (4 x 1¼ in) metal crumpet rings well with melted clarified butter.

Heat two non-stick frying pans over a low heat and add a spoonful of melted clarified butter to each. Divide the crumpet rings evenly between the pans and spoon batter into each ring until they are three-quarters filled. Allow the mixture to slowly heat in the pan for approximately 3–4 minutes. During this time you should see the characteristic holes form on the top of the batter. Once the batter looks set, carefully remove the rings, turn over the crumpets and cook the other side until browned, about 2 minutes.

Remove the crumpets from the pan and spread generously with the cultured butter. Top each with a few spoonfuls of ocean trout caviar and serve.

Jagallo Nero Kale

FAMILY
BRASSICACEAE

SPECIES
BRASSICA OLERACEA VAR. **ACEPHALA**

CULTIVAR
JAGALLO NERO

A cut-leaf variety of cavalo nero (a black Italian cabbage), Jagallo Nero has deeply indented blue-grey leaves that randomly spiral and curl. These visually striking leaves are much smaller than traditional cavolo nero leaves (though they have a similar flavour) and can be cut as required from the stem and side branches without the need for harvesting the whole plant. —— Botanically speaking, Jagallo Nero is on the kale branch of the *Brassicaceae* family, which originated in the Eastern Mediterranean and Asia Minor. It is related to other brassicas, such as broccoli, cauliflower and cabbage. A primitive member of the family, it belongs to the 'acephala' group, which means it grows without the central head typical of many varieties of cabbage. —— In Europe, kale (the name itself is Scottish, derived from the Greek word *coles* or the Roman *caulis)* was the most common green vegetable until the end of the Middle Ages and is one of the easiest vegetables to grow. Being very hardy, it will tolerate most conditions and soil types, though it does appreciate good drainage. Kale is best planted in autumn to allow it to mature in cold, winter weather. It tolerates frosts well and is generally the sweeter for it. As with any brassica, however, be mindful not to grow it in the same ground more than once every four years so as not to run the risk of clubroot infestation – a soil-borne disease that infects the roots of cruciferous plants, causing stunted growth and premature crop ripening.

Peter Gilmore

WILD BARRAMUNDI, ROASTED CABBAGE CREAM, JAGALLO NERO, SEAWEED, BROWN BUTTER

SERVES 8

In this dish the Jagallo Nero kale plays a supporting role to the wild barramundi, combining with wakame seaweed to create the appearance of a lush seabed. The roasted cabbage cream earths the dish, reinforcing the kale's flavour.

ROASTED CABBAGE CREAM

300 g (10½ oz) unsalted butter
50 g (1¾ oz) finely diced shallot
10 g (¼ oz/1 tablespoon) finely diced garlic
100 g (3½ oz) inner celery stalk, finely diced
100 ml (3½ fl oz) double-reduced Chicken Stock
    (see Basics, page 240)
1 hispi or oxheart cabbage head, green outer leaves discarded
    and white inner leaves separated
1 teaspoon lemon juice
zest of ½ lemon
sea salt

Melt 50 g (1¾ oz) of the unsalted butter in a small saucepan, add the shallot, garlic and celery and gently sauté until softened but not coloured. Add the reduced chicken stock and bring to the boil, then remove from the heat and set aside.

Wash and dry the inner cabbage leaves. Working in batches, sauté the cabbage leaves in a saucepan with the rest of the butter until golden brown. Transfer the leaves to a food processor, leaving behind any liquid in the pan, add the garlic, shallot and stock mixture and blitz on high speed to a purée. Pass through a fine-mesh sieve, add the lemon juice, lemon zest and sea salt to taste and refrigerate until needed.

Additional ingredients

250 g (9 oz) Brown Butter (see Basics, page 240)
50 ml (1¾ fl oz) olive oil
50 g (1¾ oz) unsalted butter
8 x 150 g (5½ oz) trimmed wild barramundi fillets, skin on
sea salt
about 80 Jagallo Nero kale sprigs
2 tablespoons shredded dried wakame seaweed, soaked in cold
    water for 1–2 hours and patted dry
about 20 kailan flowers

To serve

Place a large saucepan of salted water on the stove and bring to the boil. Preheat the oven to 200°C (400°F). Gently reheat the cabbage cream and warm the brown butter.

Place two non-stick frying pans over a high heat and add some olive oil and unsalted butter to each pan. Season the barramundi with sea salt and place the fish fillets, skin side down, in the frying pans. Sauté for 1½–2 minutes, until the skin is well coloured, then turn the fish over and sauté for a further minute. Place the fillets on a baking tray and finish cooking in the oven for 2–3 minutes, depending on the thickness of the fish.

Meanwhile, blanch the kale in the boiling water for 10 seconds. Drain and dress liberally with brown butter and sea salt.

Remove the fish from the oven and drain on paper towel. Place a generous spoonful of cabbage cream on the centre of each serving plate, lay over the fish fillets, skin side up, then arrange the kale and seaweed on top of the fish. Dress with the rest of the brown butter, garnish with kailan flowers and serve immediately.

Melonette Jaspee Squash

FAMILY

CUCURBITACEAE

SPECIES

CUCURBITA PEPO

CULTIVAR

MELONETTE JASPEE DE VENDEE

Melonette Jaspee de Vendee (also referred to as Melonette Saint-Julien de Croncles) is a star of the winter squash family being, quite simply, one of the sweetest, most delicious and fine-textured squashes you can grow. Part of the *Cucurbita pepo* species, which includes zucchini and other summer squash, this variety originated from the Vendee region in western France. Traditionally used in sweet dishes of all kinds, such as cakes and jams, but also in soups and even raw in salads, it is a gorgeous yellow-gold, finely embroidered squash about the size of a small melon, making it the perfect-sized squash for two. —— Melonette Jaspee should be planted in late spring, once all dangers of frost have passed, with the mature squash ready to harvest three months later from productive vines that, in my experience, can produce up to ten fruit each. When harvesting, the vines should be allowed to die back before picking so that the squash have the chance to fully develop and absorb as many nutrients as possible first. Melonette Jaspee stores well, with its flavour actually developing and improving with age. —— I first grew Melonette Jaspee on a small scale as a test of several different varieties two years ago. It was definitely a standout and this year I have grown it on a much larger scale through Erika and Hayden of Epicurean Harvest (see page 89) to use as a delicious filling for tortellini.

TORTELLINI OF ROASTED MELONETTE JASPEE SQUASH

When you have such an intensely flavourful vegetable like the Melonette Jaspee de Vendee you want to serve it with as little adornment as possible. Here, I have roasted it and simply wrapped it in an egg yolk–rich pasta and lightly dressed it in brown butter.

500 g (1 lb 2 oz) rock salt
1 Melonette Jaspee de Vendee squash (approx. 750 g/1 lb 11 oz)
50 ml (1¾ fl oz) extra-virgin olive oil
sea salt
250 g (9 oz) good-quality 00 pasta flour, plus extra for dusting
10 egg yolks
1 whole egg
100 g (3½ oz) unsalted butter, softened
1 egg, beaten
100 ml (3½ fl oz) Brown Butter (see Basics, page 241)

Preheat the oven to 160°C (320°F) and cover a baking tray in a layer of rock salt.

Cut the squash in half and remove the seeds. Brush the flesh with olive oil and lightly season with sea salt. Place the squash halves, flesh side up, on the rock salt and bake for about 1½ hours, or until the flesh is soft and lightly coloured.

Meanwhile, make the pasta dough by adding the flour and a pinch of salt to the bowl of an electric mixer fitted with the dough hook attachment. Add the egg yolks and whole egg and knead until just combined, then tip the dough out onto a lightly floured work surface and knead for approximately 10 minutes, or until smooth and elastic. Roll the dough into a ball, wrap in plastic wrap and leave to rest at room temperature for 1 hour.

Once the squash is cooked, carefully spoon out the flesh from the skin into a bowl. Stir through the softened butter and season to taste with salt, then pass the mixture through a fine-mesh drum sieve. Transfer to a bowl and leave to chill in the refrigerator.

Using a benchtop pasta machine, roll out the pasta dough on the thinnest setting. Cut into sheets and cover with a dry tea towel (dish towel) to prevent the pasta from drying out. Working one sheet at a time, and keeping the remainder covered, cut the sheet into circles using a 7 cm (2¾ in) round cutter. Place a teaspoon of the squash mixture in the centre of one of the pasta circles and brush the edge of half the circle with a little beaten egg, then fold the pasta over to create a half-moon shape and press to seal the edge firm. Holding the half-moon shape in one hand, connect the two far edges with a pinch of your thumb, then fold over the middle to form a classic tortellini shape. Repeat with the remaining pasta and filling, placing the finished tortellini onto a lightly floured baking sheet. (The tortellini will keep, refrigerated, for up to 1 hour.)

When ready to serve, bring a large saucepan of salted water to the boil and warm the brown butter in a separate pan. Add the tortellini to the boiling water and cook for 1 minute. Drain well, coat in the warm brown butter and serve immediately.

Mangel Beetroot (Mangelwurzel)

FAMILY

CHENOPODIACEAE (AMARANTHACEAE)

SPECIES

BETA VULGARIS

CULTIVAR

RED MAMMOTH

Beetroots are generally divided into three groups: Swiss chard, which is grown for its large leaves and fleshy stems, and used as a leaf vegetable; sugar beets, which, like sugar cane, are grown and refined into a source of sucrose and now provide almost half the world's sugar; and edible root beetroots, which are grown for their fleshy, swollen roots and edible leaves. These three varieties all derive from the wild sea beet *B. vulgaris* var. *maritima*, which was known to the Greeks and Romans; they consumed the leaves both as a food source and for medicinal purposes. ——— There are many modern varieties of edible root beetroot, most possessing turnip-sized swollen roots and a deep red colour, although there are also varieties that are golden yellow and pure white (not to mention one of the more unusual varieties, the candy stripe, or Chioggia, beetroot from Italy). Growing beetroot requires full sun and regular watering, as well as free-draining, well-composted soil. The best crops are produced in spring and autumn as they prefer mild to warm conditions – excessively hot weather is not suitable. ——— Mangel beetroot, also known as mangelwurzel, were developed in the 1700s as a nutritious source of livestock fodder; these beets grew extremely large and were considered too coarse for human consumption. I first decided to grow the Red Mammoth mangel beetroot for its impressive size and discovered that, as a very young beet, it makes a very worthy culinary ingredient, being both delightfully tender and possessing an attractive pink hue.

ROASTED YOUNG RED MAMMOTH MANGEL BEETROOT, DORY ROE EMULSION

SERVES 8

Although the Red Mammoth mangel beetroot is fibrous when it grows to its full, astonishing size, when picked very young (at about the size of a small carrot) I have found it to be sweet and tender. Here, I have treated it simply – roasting it on a bed of rock salt, then peeling it and dressing it with olive oil. The mirror dory roe emulsion provides a good foil for the beetroot's earthy flavour.

1 kg (2 lb 3 oz) rock salt
8 small Red Mammoth mangel beetroot
320 ml (11 fl oz) extra-virgin olive oil, plus extra to serve
1 garlic clove, finely diced
3 egg yolks
1 teaspoon lemon juice
250 g (9 oz) fresh mirror dory roe or other fish roe
1 teaspoon lemon zest
sea salt
8 flowering buckwheat sprigs

Preheat the oven to 180°C (350°F) and cover a baking tray in a layer of rock salt.

Wash the beetroot thoroughly and trim off the leaves. Place the beetroot on the rock salt and roast for 45 minutes, or until the beetroot are tender when pierced with the point of a sharp knife. Remove from the oven and let cool, then peel off the skins and set aside until needed.

Meanwhile, warm 200 ml (7 fl oz) of the olive oil in a small saucepan to 50°C (120°F). Add the garlic, remove the pan from the heat and leave for 1 hour to cool completely.

Add the egg yolks and lemon juice to a food processor and whiz together, slowly drizzling in the cooled garlic-infused oil as you go, until well emulsified. Squeeze out any excess moisture from the fish roe, then add it to the food processor and blitz together briefly to combine. Press the mixture through a fine-mesh drum sieve into a bowl, add the lemon zest and season to taste with sea salt, then transfer to the refrigerator and leave to chill for at least 1 hour.

When ready to serve, dress the beetroot with the remaining olive oil and a sprinkling of sea salt. Place a spoonful of the roe emulsion on each plate and spread it out with the back of a spoon, then top each with a dressed beetroot and a sprig of flowering buckwheat. Drizzle over a little extra-virgin olive oil and serve.

FIONA WEIR WALMSLEY
AND ADAM WALMSLEY

BUENA VISTA FARM

Fiona Weir Walmsley and her husband, Adam, run a small farm on the New South Wales South Coast. Their mixed farm approach is one that I find very inspiring. It is an approach that I would one day love to adopt myself for supplying my own country restaurant, one where you can come close to being as self-sufficient as possible. Although I work very closely with great farmers to supply my city restaurants, to be even closer to the source – in fact to be part of the process itself – is a dream I hope to achieve. Fiona and Adam's integrated approach sees them produce wonderful organic vegetables, their own honey, their own milk for cheesemaking, as well as their own grass-fed beef and pastured poultry, with them then adding value to these products in various ways.

The story of Buena Vista Farm is told by Fiona –

Buena Vista Farm is in Gerringong, right on the coast and two hours south of Sydney. It's a small farm now – part of what was a larger family farm – and we are dedicated to practising small-scale sustainable agriculture and encouraging people to make connections with where their food comes from. We're passionate about strong local food systems and about nutrient-dense, handmade whole foods being a part of everyday kitchens. I grew up on the farm but left after high school to go to university in Sydney, and then to travel and work. My husband, Adam, and I made our way back to Gerringong in 2012 after my dad retired, and set about building a farm and food business.

Buena Vista has been in my family since the 1850s, when my Irish great great grandfather and grandmother arrived on a boat in Sydney Harbour, travelled slowly down to the new township of Gerringong and rented this piece of land from Alexander Berry. When it eventually came up for sale after the Berry brothers both died, my great great grandfather rode his horse into the auction in Kiama (after milking!) and successfully bid on the farm he'd been tending for twenty-five years.

This place was always a dairy farm until Dad retired, sold the herd and shut down the dairy. When Adam and I decided to take the plunge, abandon our city lives and move home to Gerringong, we were heavily influenced by the work of Joel Salatin and inspired to have a go at a mixed farming enterprise. We now raise free-range pigs, grass-fed cattle, pastured poultry (eggs and meat) and dairy goats, keep bees and have an organic veggie garden that supplies our local weekly farmers' market as well as several local restaurants. Our market gardener, Emmy King, works her magic full-time in the garden, and produces a huge amount of veg, from a 900 m (2950 ft) square plot. (The soil is pretty amazing, we're very lucky.)

We built a commercial kitchen early on so we could add value to our eggs and veggies, as well as turning some of the less pretty produce into pickles and krauts. We teach cooking classes every weekend, featuring traditional foods and skills like sourdough baking, fermenting and cheesemaking.

It's a lot of work and a lot of fun – we eat like kings and get to sit on grassy green hills overlooking the ocean while feeling extremely lucky to be here, growing food. One of the things about an old family farm is that you carry a strong sense of the long line of people acting as stewards of the land. You're just responsible for this moment in time – there were people before you doing their best, and there'll be people after you doing theirs too. No one really owns it, or is solely in charge, rather we are reliant on good people working with us just like my grandfather and his grandfather were, and those that follow us will be too. In the meantime, there's sourdough fresh from the oven served with hand-churned cultured butter, crisp just-picked salad leaves topped with homemade goat's cheese and some of last year's tomato chilli jam. Life is delicious.

White Sprouting Broccoli

FAMILY
BRASSICACEAE

SPECIES
BRASSICA OLERACEA VAR. F. ALBIDA

CULTIVAR
WHITE EYE

Sprouting broccoli is a vegetable more commonly known in its purple or green form, however the white is the sweetest and most delicately flavoured of all. There is a beauty to it that is so evocative of spring and new growth – a tender sweetness after a cold winter and a sign of the bounty yet to come. —— Sprouting broccoli is a member of the *Brassicaceae* family, one of the largest families of vegetables we consume. Originating from a wild cabbage plant found in the Mediterranean and Asia Minor region, along with the broccolis *Brassicaceae* counts cabbages, cauliflowers, brussels sprouts, kale, turnips, kohlrabi, rutabaga and mustards among its members – it is amazing to me that all these varieties originate from a single wild plant, with numerous cultivars and hybrids continuing to be developed. Though there is evidence that an early form of broccoli was known to the Greeks 2500 years ago, present-day varieties have been developed principally from broccolis grown in Italy over the past 2000 years (the word broccoli means 'little sprouts' in Italian, which makes sense when referring to sprouting broccoli). —— In countries with long, harsh winters, sprouting broccoli is normally planted out in late spring after the frosts have gone. It is grown for almost a full year – the plant will need to be staked and protected over winter – and in the following early spring you will be rewarded with a flourish of white sprouts. I have found that in Australia, with our milder winters, I can plant out young seedlings in early autumn to achieve a harvest that spring, eliminating the length of time the plant needs to be in the ground. When harvesting, it is best to remove the central floret first to encourage the side shoots to sprout. —— What I love about white sprouting broccoli, apart from its delicate flavour, is its sheer beauty – the contrast between its white flowering heads and light green leaves is striking – along with its availability in the garden during a period when little else is going on. If continually picked, you can be harvesting this vegetable for at least six weeks, making it worth the wait. A couple of cultivars I have grown are the early sprouting White Eye and the late sprouting White Star, both sourced from Seedaholic in Ireland; planting both will help extend your broccoli season even further.

WHITE SPROUTING BROCCOLI, WILD GREEN-LIPPED ABALONE, BROWN BUTTER EMULSION

SERVES 8

White sprouting broccoli is one of my all-time favourite vegetables, and its delicate, sweet flavour and striking appearance makes it the perfect accompaniment to seafood delicacies. In this dish I have combined it with green-lipped abalone, together with a sauce whose delicious sharp, fermented flavour – beautifully tempered by the addition of brown butter – brings out the best qualities of both ingredients. There is no doubt this is a luxurious dish (albeit a deceptively simple-looking one) where the stars of the show are the top-quality ingredients.

NOTE: *The salting of the cabbage leaves for the fermented cabbage and brown butter emulsion needs to be done 4 days in advance of cooking, while the brown butter aïoli should be made just before serving. You can buy green-lipped abalone already cleaned and frozen or live in the shell – if opting for the latter, use a 350–400 g (12½–14 oz) green-lipped abalone or two smaller 200 g (7 oz) ones and clean thoroughly before use.*

FERMENTED CABBAGE AND BROWN BUTTER EMULSION

400 g (14 oz) white cabbage heart, leaves separated
2 teaspoons sea salt
100 ml (3½ fl oz) Brown Butter (see Basics, page 241)

Add the cabbage leaves to a vacuum-seal bag, sprinkle over the salt and seal the bag, removing all the air. Leave the bag at room temperature for 4 days to allow the cabbage to ferment naturally. After 4 days, remove the cabbage leaves from the bag, discarding any liquid, transfer to an electric juicer and juice. Pass the juice through a fine-mesh sieve. Measure out 200 ml (7 fl oz) of the strained juice, add to a saucepan with the brown butter and simmer over a high heat until reduced by half. Set aside.

BROWN BUTTER AÏOLI

150 ml (5 fl oz) extra-virgin olive oil
1 garlic clove, finely diced
100 ml (3½ fl oz) Brown Butter (see Basics, page 241), melted
4 egg yolks
zest of ¼ lemon
sea salt

Warm the olive oil in a saucepan to 50°C (120°F). Add the garlic, remove the pan from the heat and leave to infuse for 1 hour. Strain, discarding the garlic pieces.

In a bowl, combine the brown butter with the garlic-infused extra-virgin olive oil and whisk together well. Add the egg yolks to a separate bowl and slowly drizzle over the oil and butter mixture, whisking all the while, until fully incorporated. Add the lemon zest and salt to taste.

Additional ingredients

60 white sprouting broccoli florets
(approx. 500 g/1 lb 2 oz), trimmed
200 g (7 oz) cleaned green-lipped abalone,
defrosted
250 ml (8½ fl oz/1 cup) melted unsalted butter

To serve

Warm the fermented cabbage and brown butter emulsion in a small saucepan. Blanch the broccoli in a large saucepan of boiling water for 1 minute. Drain and keep warm.

Using a sharp filleting knife, slice the abalone as thinly as possible. Heat the melted butter in a saucepan to 70°C (160°F), add the abalone and poach briefly for 30–40 seconds, or until the flesh is opaque. Drain.

Place a couple of spoonfuls of the brown butter aïoli in the centre of individual warmed serving plates. Top with the broccoli florets and abalone slices and spoon over the warmed emulsion. Serve.

Oxheart Tomato

FAMILY

SOLANACEAE

SPECIES

SOLANUM LYCOPERSICUM

CULTIVAR

OXHEART

The heavenly scent of a tomato vine in the height of summer, once experienced, is not easily forgotten, and the pleasure of growing tomatoes in your back garden is one that is now appreciated by many cultures around the world. —— The tomato originated in central and western south America and, while the exact date of domestication is unknown, by 500 BC it was being cultivated in southern Mexico by the Aztecs and other Mesoamerican peoples. The Spanish conquistador Hernan Cortes may have been the first to transfer the small yellow tomato to Europe after he captured the Aztec city of Tenochtitlán, now Mexico City, in 1521, though there are some reports that Christopher Columbus may have brought them back as early as 1493. Regardless, after the Spanish colonisation of the Americas, the Spanish distributed the tomato throughout their colonies in the Caribbean and the Philippines; from there they spread to Southeast Asia and then the entire Asian continent. —— Initially tomatoes, like other plants in the nightshade family such as the potato, were greeted with suspicion in Europe, as they were believed to be poisonous. (In fact, while the leaves and stems of the tomato are alkaloid-rich and slightly poisonous, the fruit is not.) Slowly, the merits of the tomato gained acceptance and its popularity grew, with the tomato's ability to mutate and create new and different varieties contributing to its success and helping it spread throughout Italy in particular. Unique varieties were developed over the next few centuries for different uses such as drying, cooking and sauce-making as well as fresh eating, and it is now almost impossible to imagine Italian cuisine without the tomato. —— These days, there is a clear gap that exists between tomatoes grown for commerce and those grown for pleasure. Modern commercial hybrids tend to be bred primarily not for flavour but for factors like consistent size, shape, disease and pest resistance as well as suitability for mechanised picking and shipping, with an ability to ripen after picking. Some of this can be put down to the breeding of tomatoes to ripen uniformly red. This change occurred after the discovery of the mutant (u) phenotype in the mid-20th century that ripened uniformly red. This was widely crossbred to produce red fruit without the typical green shoulder around the stem. Since then, evidence has shown that the green shoulders help to fix carbon within the fruit through photosynthesis; therefore they produce up to fifteen per cent more sugar during ripening, and thus a more intensely flavoured tomato. As a result, non-uniformly red heirloom varieties are popular among home gardeners as they tend to produce more interesting and highly flavoured tomatoes. —— Each summer season I like to experiment with as many different tomato varieties as possible, as there are new ones being developed all the time. Often, though, it is hard to go past the classic heirloom varieties such as Brandywine and Oxheart – those large, intensely flavoured tomatoes with small seed pockets, with the latter being one of my all-time favourites.

PETER GILMORE

SLOW-ROASTED OXHEART TOMATO, FRESH BUFFALO MILK BURRATA, REDUCED MADEIRA, KAMPOT PEPPER

SERVES 8

One of the classic heirloom tomato varieties, Oxhearts are very compact, solid tomatoes with an intense, rich flavour. Here, I have slowly dehydrated the tomatoes over about eight hours to concentrate that flavour – which is complemented by the reduced Madeira – while the kampot pepper provides a nice level of heat that contrasts well with the soft, milky burrata. These tomatoes could be served at room temperature, but I prefer them a little chilled.

8 medium Oxheart tomatoes
100 ml (3½ fl oz) extra-virgin olive oil, plus extra for brushing and drizzling
sea salt
500 ml (17 fl oz/2 cups) good-quality dry Madeira
2 teaspoons kampot peppercorns
8 fresh buffalo milk burrata or mozzarella balls

Bring a large saucepan of salted water to the boil and have a large bowl of iced water on standby.

Carefully score a small cross on top of each tomato. Lower the tomatoes into the saucepan of boiling water and blanch for 30 seconds, then transfer directly to the bowl of iced water. Leave the tomatoes for 1 minute to refresh, then remove them from the iced water and carefully peel away the skins.

Place the peeled tomatoes on a fine-mesh wire rack, brush with a little olive oil and sprinkle with salt. Transfer the rack to a dehydrator or a very low oven preheated to 50°C (120°F) and dehydrate for 6–8 hours, or until the tomatoes are wrinkly and reduced in size by about one-third but still juicy inside. Leave the tomatoes to cool completely, then refrigerate for a minimum of 1 hour to chill slightly.

Meanwhile, reduce the Madeira in a small saucepan over a low heat until you have about 100 ml (3½ fl oz) remaining. Whisk the extra-virgin olive oil into the reduced Madeira with a pinch of sea salt until emulsified. Remove from the heat and set aside to cool to room temperature.

In a mortar and pestle, grind the kampot peppercorns to a fine powder. Remove the tomatoes from the refrigerator, dress each with a teaspoon or so of the Madeira dressing and season generously with the freshly ground kampot pepper.

Carefully place one of the dressed tomatoes on an individual serving plate and sit a fresh buffalo milk burrata alongside it. Repeat with the remaining tomatoes and burrata, dressing each cheese with a drizzle of extra-virgin olive oil and a sprinkling of sea salt. Finish each tomato with a final drizzle of the Madeira dressing and serve.

Gagon Cucumber

FAMILY
CUCURBITACEAE

SPECIES
CUCUMIS SATIVUS

CULTIVAR
GAGON

With its beautiful rusty red speckled skin when fully mature, the Gagon cucumber resembles the Indian Poona Keera heirloom cucumber, though it is much larger and is even more striking. A rare variety originating in Bhutan, the cucumbers are traditionally grown to full maturity to a length of up to 40 cm (16 in), and the flesh of the mature fruit is more reminiscent of a melon than a typical cucumber, albeit a little firmer and less sweet. Traditionally, Gagon cucumbers are cooked and are typically braised in a similar fashion to the way winter melons are treated in Chinese cuisine. —— It's not surprising that there are cucumbers like Gagon and Poona Keera that look similar from different parts of the world as there are literally thousands of cucumber cultivars in existence. Cucumbers were first brought under cultivation in the Indus Valley some 3000 years ago before spreading to China and other parts of Asia. The ancient Greeks were the first Europeans to cultivate cucumbers, while the Romans made crock pickles with cucumbers very similar to those prepared by the Germans and eastern Europeans today. —— The Gagon cucumber's seeds were originally collected in 1981 from the Trongsa district of Bhutan. I obtained the seed for this rare cucumber from Baker Creek Heirloom Seeds and have had success growing it in my garden in Sydney. The cucumbers are generally not grown on a trellis and are at their best when given room for the vine to spread over the ground (in a similar way to melons) and when planted on slightly heaped mounds, which help their roots to drain. Gagon starts flowering and fruiting from about eight weeks – when the cucumbers first form they are small and pale green and can be eaten fresh or used as pickles. It takes a further three to four weeks for them to reach full maturity, though even when fully mature, the seed cavity is relatively small for its size, leaving a good amount of thick flesh. The fruit tends to form close to the base of the plants initially but will continue to form further along the vines. It's a joy to see these large, rusty red, exotic-looking cucumbers growing in the garden.

BRAISE OF GAGON CUCUMBER,
GREEN-LIPPED ABALONE, SHIMONITA ONION

SERVES 8

This dish combines the Gagon cucumber with shimonita onion and green-lipped abalone, as is traditional in Bhutan, slow-braising the ingredients in a complex umami-laden stock.

2 x 200 g (7 oz) fresh green-lipped abalone
1 large Gagon cucumber
1 litre (34 fl oz/4 cups) Umami Stock (see Basics, page 240)
3 shimonita onions
50 g (1¾ oz) unsalted butter
extra-virgin olive oil
sea salt

Shuck the abalones, remove the intestines and cut away the tough outer frills. Dice the abalone flesh into 3 cm (1¼ in) pieces and set aside until required.

Using a vegetable peeler or paring knife, scrape away most of the outer skin of the Gagon cucumber, leaving behind just a trace of the red skin. Cut the cucumber in half lengthways and remove the seeds, then cut the flesh into 3 cm (1¼ in) cubes.

Pour the umami stock into a heavy-based saucepan set over a high heat, bring to a simmer and leave for 10–15 minutes, or until the stock has reduced by about half.

Peel and discard the outer layers from the shimonita onions and slice the remainder into 3 cm (1¼ in) rounds. Add to a heavy-based saucepan together with the cucumber, butter and reduced stock, bring to a gentle simmer and cook over a low heat, stirring as you go, for 10 minutes, or until the stock and butter have reduced to form a glaze and the cucumber and onion are soft.

Meanwhile, heat a charcoal barbecue grill or large non-stick frying pan until very hot.

Brush the abalone with a little oil, then transfer to the hot grill or frying pan and sauté briefly until lightly golden, about 1–2 minutes on each side.

Add the abalone to the saucepan, stir to coat in the glaze and simmer for a further minute. Season to taste with sea salt, divide among bowls and serve.

Bear Necessities Kale

FAMILY
BRASSICACEAE

SPECIES
BRASSICA NAPUS

CULTIVAR
BEAR NECESSITIES

Bear Necessities kale was developed by plant breeder Tim Peters. Derived from Russian and Siberian kales (*B. napus*) and crossed with mizuna (*B. rapa*), this special kale's super-frilly, serrated leaves, which vary in colour from green to red, truly help it to stand out from the rest of the kale pack. —— Russian and Siberian kales are super-hardy winter survivalists whose leaves, after the first frosts, sweeten dramatically and are generally more tender than most of the European kales (*B. oleracea*). These species are thought to have originated from a chance hybridisation between other brassica species in European gardens during the Middle Ages. Indeed, in developing Bear Necessities and other brassicas, Tim retraced their evolution himself by crossing a Chinese cabbage (*B. rapa*) with a European kale (*B. oleracea*) using the bud pollination technique, with this cross resulting in a beautiful Siberian kale (*B. napus*). He then crossed in black mustard (*B. nigra*) and this resulted in the red Russian kale (*B. napus*), with its distinctive colour and leaf shapes proving that some of the *B. napus* species are two-way mix-ups and some are three-way mix-ups – a powerful demonstration of man's ingenuity and powers of observation, which have allowed this flourishing of diversity that goes hand in hand with nature's own evolutionary process. —— I was first introduced to Bear Necessities kale by Dylan and Elle, of Newcastle Greens, who were the first to grow this kale in Australia. I was curious about its name and even more delighted by its appearance and flavour. I asked Elle to find out how the name 'Bear Necessities' came about; she contacted Tim Peters directly and he told her the story of its development and how he came up with the name as a playful reference to its Russian heritage.

BEAR NECESSITIES KALE, SASHIMI BLUE MACKEREL, EGGPLANT, PERILLA, SESAME

SERVES 8

In this recipe, I use the kale as a crispy foil to the succulent sashimi mackerel, which is seasoned with virgin soy sauce, black-rice vinegar and sesame oil. The smoked eggplant cream adds another dimension to the dish, as does the final addition of crunchy perilla and sesame seeds.

8 large Bear Necessities kale leaves
1 litre (34 fl oz/4 cups) grapeseed oil
sea salt
3 x 300 g (10½ oz) sashimi-grade blue (slimy) mackerel, skinned, filleted and cut into 1 cm (½ in) cubes
50 ml (1¾ fl oz) virgin soy sauce
2 teaspoons black-rice vinegar
50 ml (1¾ fl oz) toasted sesame oil
30 g (1 oz/3 tablespoons) toasted white sesame seeds
30 g (1 oz/3 tablespoons) toasted perilla seeds
125 ml (4 fl oz/½ cup) Smoked Eggplant Cream (see Basics, page 241)

Bring a large saucepan of salted water to the boil and have a large bowl of iced water on standby. Blanch each kale leaf individually in the boiling water for 5 seconds, then immediately refresh in the iced water. Drain the leaves and pat dry, then dehydrate in a dehydrator or a very low oven preheated to 80°C (175°F) for 3 hours, or until dry and crinkly.

In a large heavy-based saucepan, heat the grapeseed oil to 160°C (320°F). Deep-fry the dehydrated kale leaves, one by one, in the hot oil until golden and crispy, about 15–20 seconds. Drain well on paper towel and season with sea salt. Set aside.

Toss the mackerel pieces together with the soy sauce to cover evenly. Leave the mackerel to macerate for 20 seconds, then strain to remove any excess soy. Transfer the mackerel to a clean bowl.

Whisk together the black rice-vinegar and toasted sesame oil to combine and pour over the mackerel. Add half the toasted sesame and perilla seeds and toss together well.

Divide the kale leaves among serving plates and top each with a tablespoon of the eggplant cream. Pile over a large tablespoon of the dressed mackerel pieces and sprinkle over the remaining perilla and sesame seeds. Serve.

Tropean Red Onion

FAMILY
AMARYLLIDACEAE

SPECIES
ALLIUM CEPA

CULTIVAR
CIPOLLA ROSSA DI TROPEA

Italy boasts many varieties of onions, but perhaps the most famously appreciated are the sweet red onions of Tropea. Beloved for their unique sweetness, delicate scent, refined taste and crisp texture, they can be round or oval in shape and are excellent raw in salads or cooked in numerous ways; with their high sugar content they caramelise beautifully and are traditionally made into a delicious marmalade, for example. Grown in an area that stretches in both directions along the coast from Tropea in Calabria, these onions have been cultivated in this particular region for more than 2000 years, having been introduced to the area by the Phoenicians, who themselves inherited them from the Assyrians and Babylonians before them. —— Traditionally these onions were grown by hand on the clay cliffs that descend from Mount Poro towards the sea between Capo Vaticano, Zambrone, Tropea and Briatico, and the climatic conditions, soil, temperature, humidity and hours of sunlight contribute to its sublime physical and chemical composition. Historically, Tropean red onions have been the most valuable crop of the area (their name is a result of the fact that shipment of the onions to various ports around the world took place from the railway station of Tropea) and today the crop still contributes to the socio-economic prosperity of the region, as well as playing a role in the identity and traditions of the local cuisine, which helps to attract gastronomic tourists. Cipolla Rossa di Tropea obtained IGP (Protected Geographic Identification) status in 2008, with the onions even having their own festival, held in Ricadi, every year in August. —— For the home gardener, these sweet onions can be sown in autumn if you have mild winter conditions, but are otherwise best sown in spring in soil that has been enriched with well-rotted organic matter (onions don't like to compete with weeds, so mulching is useful); they are best harvested when the bulbs are mature and the foliage has turned yellow. At this point you should stop watering and pull back the covering of earth or mulch to expose the bulbs' surface to the sun and leave them for about two weeks in the soil before carefully lifting them with a fork. While the onions store well in a cool, well-lit place for up to three months with their flavour remaining sweet, I find that they are at their most delicious when consumed fresh from the garden.

TARTE TATIN OF TROPEAN RED ONIONS

SERVES 8

Tropean red onions are so sweet that they lend themselves well to this slightly savoury take on the classic tarte tatin. Served simply with the accompanying dill crème fraîche and a salad, these individual tarts are perfect for lunch.

16 small Tropean red onions, peeled
2 tablespoons grapeseed oil
sea salt
100 g (3½ oz) caster (superfine) sugar
50 g (1¾ oz) unsalted butter, diced and at room temperature
2 sheets good-quality butter puff pastry
1 small bunch dill, fronds picked
250 g (7 oz) crème fraîche

Preheat the oven to 180°C (350°F).

Coat the onions in the grapeseed oil and season lightly with sea salt. Lay them on a sheet of baking paper and wrap them up to form a parcel, then transfer to a wire rack in the oven and bake for 10 minutes.

Add the sugar to a heavy-based saucepan set over a high heat. Once the sugar caramelises to a deep golden caramel, add the butter and stir until the butter is melted and well combined. Take off the heat. Pour about a tablespoon of the caramel over each of the bases of eight oval-shaped tart moulds.

Lay two precooked onions, top to tail, into each mould over the caramel. Roll out the puff pastry sheets to a 5 mm (¼ in) thickness and prick the pastry all over with a fork, then cut the pastry into roughly the same shape as the moulds. Place the pastry over the onions and tuck in the edges. Bake the tarts for approximately 15 minutes, until the pastry looks golden brown. Remove the tarts from the oven, place a plate over the top of one of the tarts and invert it to remove the tart from the mould. Repeat with the remaining tarts and leave to cool slightly.

Meanwhile, combine the dill fronds with the crème fraîche. Serve the tarts warm, sprinkled with a pinch of sea salt and with a spoonful of the dill crème fraîche on the side.

Agretti

FAMILY
CHENOPODIACEAE

SPECIES
SALSOLA SODA

Agretti is a famed vegetable in Italy, where it is also referred to as '*barba di frate*' or 'monk's beard' – a name that comes from its association with the Capuchin monks, who were well known for growing it. It is often mistaken for the land seaweed okahijiki (*Salsola komarovi*), a similar-looking plant (and, incidentally, one of Japan's oldest vegetables), which, like agretti, is a halophyte (a plant that has adapted to grow in areas of high salinity) along with other coastal plants such as samphire, sea aster, sea beet, saltbush and Warrigal greens. —— Historically, agretti was harvested as an important source for the production of soda ash – a substance crucial in glass- and soap-making. The famed clarity of 16th-century cristallo glass from Murano was dependent upon the purity of the soda ash extracted from the burnt ashes of agretti. Today, agretti is enjoying a renewal of popularity for its culinary properties, which is no surprise given its fine-structured leaves and succulent, crunchy texture. —— I first looked into growing agretti a few years back after I first tasted it in Italy, and the process took a number of years. Though it is possible to grow agretti (and other halophytes) in regular soil, it has a notoriously low germination rate, while the seed is also difficult to obtain and needs to be as fresh as possible, only proving viable for about six months. In my first year of growing agretti I planted over 300 seeds and got just two plants to take – but, once these plants came into seed, I was able to share the fresh seed with one of my growers and we finally had a successful crop.

GRILLED SARDINES, AGRETTI, LEMON ZEST, CAPERS

SERVES 8

This Italian seaside succulent vegetable is one of my favourite greens. Here, it is matched with fresh, oily sardines and a simple dressing of lemon and capers – its grassy, salty, herbaceous flavour cuts through the richness of the fish beautifully.

16 fresh sardines, gutted and heads removed
200 ml (7 fl oz) extra-virgin olive oil
3 garlic cloves, finely sliced
2 tablespoons salted capers, rinsed
zest of 1 lemon
sea salt
32 agretti sprigs (approx. 250 g/9 oz)

Using your fingers, split open the sardines, keeping the skins intact, and remove the soft backbones and ribs (this, in effect, will butterfly the sardines). Run your fingers along the flesh to check for any remaining large bones and remove them with tweezers. Set aside.

Warm 150 ml (5 fl oz) of the olive oil in a small saucepan to about 50°C (120°F), add the garlic and leave to infuse for 10 minutes. Strain and discard the garlic, then return the oil to the pan together with the capers and lemon zest and keep warm until required.

Bring a large saucepan of salted water to the boil. Heat a charcoal barbecue grill or large non-stick frying pan until very hot.

Brush the sardines on both sides with the remaining olive oil and season with sea salt, then transfer to the hot barbecue or pan, skin side down. Cook for about 1 minute, or until well coloured, then turn the sardines over and cook for a further minute. Remove from the heat and set aside to rest.

Add the agretti to the pan of boiling water and blanch for 30 seconds. Drain, transfer to a large bowl together with the warm infused oil and mix together well.

Place a little agretti on each serving plate and top with two grilled sardines, then finish with the rest of the agretti, spooning over any remaining dressing from the bowl. Serve.

Crystal Apple Cucumber

FAMILY
CUCURBITACEAE

SPECIES
CUCUMIS SATIVUS

CULTIVAR
CRYSTAL APPLE

Although considered to be an iconic Australian heirloom, the Crystal Apple cucumber was introduced to America from Australia in 1930 by Arthur Yates & Company and is likely to have originated in China. Its small, spherical, creamy white cucumbers are about the size of a small apple and are so tender they can be eaten skin and all. —— Not technically vegetables, but fruits closely related to melons, cucumbers are thought to have originated in India as wild fruits with a distinctly bitter flavour. By the 7th century BC most of the bitterness had been bred out of the fruit to make it more palatable, after which time it migrated from India to China and Japan, where even sweeter varieties were developed. Early Roman and Greek farmers were also instrumental in increasing the varieties that were developed; according to Pliny the Elder, the emperor Tiberius had cucumber on his table daily during summer and winter. The Romans reportedly used artificial methods for cultivation similar to the greenhouse system – growing cucumber plants under frames glazed with 'mirror stone' (believed to be sheets of mica) and in houses glazed with oiled cloth known as *specularia*. Their cultivation in Europe continued during the Middle Ages, with Charlemagne growing them in his gardens in the 8th and 9th centuries. —— Cucumbers are mainly bred for two purposes: fresh eating cucumbers and smaller pickling cucumbers, and produce both male and female flowers. The female flower is swollen at its base and it is this that develops into the cucumber once pollination occurs. Cucumbers like a free-draining soil rich in nutrients and grow in full sun but prefer to be shaded for part of the day, especially during the hotter months in the tropics and subtropics. If growing outside, they should be planted in spring once the last frosts have gone. Germination is rapid, with seedlings emerging from the soil within seven to ten days of sowing. You can expect to harvest most cucumbers, including the Crystal Apple, within ten to twelve weeks of sowing. —— I have grown lots of different varieties of cucumbers, including different varieties of gherkins, small sour Mexican cucumbers and long, thin traditional Japanese cucumbers that have a rough, spiky skin but a very small, almost non-existent seed cavity. But definitely one of my favourite varieties to grow is the Crystal Apple – both for its beautiful, generous fruit and its prolific, sprawling vine.

Peter Gilmore

FLATHEAD TAIL WITH SEARED CRYSTAL APPLE CUCUMBER, REDUCED VERJUICE

SERVES 8

Although generally served raw, cucumbers are sensational when cooked like a vegetable. Here the Crystal Apple cucumbers are seared on a hot grill and dressed with a reduced verjuice, giving them a sweet, smoky tartness that goes very well with fish.

500 ml (17 fl oz/2 cups) semillon verjuice or other white verjuice
4 x 300 g (10½ oz) flathead tails on the bone, scaled
100 g (3½ oz) softened unsalted butter
sea salt
8 golf ball-sized Crystal Apple cucumbers, halved
50 ml (1¾ fl oz) grapeseed oil
25 pearl or barletta onions, peeled
30 g (1 oz) pea shoots
100 ml (3½ fl oz) melted butter

In a small heavy-based saucepan, on a very low simmer, slowly reduce the verjuice down to 80 ml (2½ fl oz/⅓ cup), or until thick with a viscosity similar to honey. Remove from the heat and set aside at room temperature until needed.

Preheat the oven to 180°C (350°F).

Using a sharp knife, cut the flathead tails below the gut area, leaving the spine of the fish intact (use the upper portions of the tails, filleted, in another dish). Lay one of the cut tails onto a 30 cm (12 in) square of baking paper, spread over one-quarter of the softened butter, and season lightly with sea salt, then roll up the paper into a bonbon shape, twisting it at each end to seal. Repeat the process with the remaining tails, transfer the parcels to a wire rack and bake in the oven for 5–6 minutes, or until the fish flesh begins to set and looks as though it will come away from the bone easily. Leave to rest for 2 minutes before cutting the flesh off the bone with a sharp knife.

Meanwhile, bring a small saucepan of water to the boil and heat a charcoal barbecue grill or grill pan until very hot. Coat the cucumber halves with the grapeseed oil, transfer them to the hot grill, cut side down, and sear for 1 minute. Set aside. Blanch the pearl onions in the saucepan of boiling water for 60 seconds, adding the pea shoots to the pan for the final 10 seconds. Drain, then dress the onions and pea shoots with the melted butter and season with sea salt.

Place a deboned fish fillet on each serving plate and arrange the seared cucumber halves, dressed onions and pea shoots alongside. Drizzle the cucumbers with the reduced verjuice and serve.

Lamborn Snap Pea Greens

FAMILY
FABACEAE

SPECIES
PISUM SATIVUM

CULTIVAR
LAMBORN SNAP PEA GREEN

The sugar-snap pea that we are familiar with today is the result of plant breeder Dr Calvin Lamborn. While working for the Gallatin Valley Seed Company in Twin Falls, Idaho, Lamborn set out to solve several problems associated with snow peas, primarily the twisting, buckling and distortion of the pods. Shown a rouge, thick-skinned shelling pea that had been found many years earlier by his colleague Dr MC Parker, Lamborn noticed, upon close inspection, that the walls of this pea were thicker than most regular shelling peas. Hoping the thick walls might counteract the twisting and buckling of the snow pea's pods, he crossed the two together, with the result being snap peas – an entirely new class of edible pea with plump, edible pods containing juicy peas that are deliciously sweet at full maturity. This original sugar snap was awarded a gold medal by the AAS (All-America Selections) seed committee in 1979, became a smash success and put both Lamborn and Gallatin Valley on the home gardener's map. —— Now considered the father of modern pea breeding, Dr Lamborn went on to breed many other varieties of pea including Lamborn Snap Pea Greens, which are grown just for their edible shoots and leaves. With their large, juicy, thick leaves and fine spindly pea tendrils that, uniquely, spread out like a fan, these are the most delicious pea greens I have ever tasted, particularly when sautéed in butter or lightly steamed and dressed with olive oil. And, while the pods of this particular variety aren't the most desired part of the plant, I have found that the peas inside the pods are quite unique in that they can be double-shelled like broad beans, with the result being an incredibly tender vegetable. —— Lamborn Snap Pea Greens can only be grown under licence with permission from the Lamborn family, and Dylan and Elle from Newcastle Greens spent more than a year communicating with Rod Lamborn, the son of Calvin, to obtain the rights and seed to grow these exceptional greens in Australia. I first came across the greens when they were entered into the *delicious.* magazine awards; I was super impressed both with them and with Dylan and Elle's commitment to growing rare and unusual varieties of edible greens, herbs and flowers.

WILTED LAMBORN SNAP PEA GREENS, PEA CUSTARD, CHICKEN AND BROWN BUTTER JUICES

SERVES 8

This dish utilises all parts of the Lamborn snap pea – the leaf tips, buds, tendrils, peas and flowers – which are then combined with a chicken stock and pea custard and finished with reduced chicken stock juices and brown butter. You can make this dish vegetarian by replacing the chicken stock with vegetable stock.

30 g (1 oz) unsalted butter
2 shallots, finely diced
1 garlic clove, finely diced
200 ml (7 fl oz) milk
1 litre (34 fl oz/4 cups) Chicken Stock (see Basics, page 240)
90 g (3 oz) Lamborn pea tendrils
5 eggs
2 tablespoons Brown Butter (see Basics, page 241)
40 Lamborn pea pods, shelled
sea salt
24 Lamborn pea leaf tips, with buds attached
50 ml (1¾ fl oz) melted unsalted butter
16 Lamborn pea flowers

Melt the butter in a heavy-based saucepan, add the shallots and garlic and sauté over a low heat until translucent. Pour the milk and 600 ml (20½ fl oz) of the chicken stock into the pan and stir to combine, then bring to a simmer over a medium heat and cook for 5 minutes. Remove from the heat and add 40 g (1½ oz) of the pea tendrils to the pan, then transfer the mixture to a blender or food processor and blitz on high speed for 30 seconds. Pour the mixture through a fine-mesh sieve and leave to cool, then measure out 600 ml (20½ fl oz) of the mixture into a bowl, add the eggs and whisk together well. Refrigerate until needed.

Add the remaining 400 ml (13½ fl oz) chicken stock to another saucepan, bring to the boil and simmer vigorously for about 5 minutes, or until reduced by half. Stir in the brown butter and return to the boil, then remove from the heat and refrigerate until needed.

Bring a large saucepan of salted water to the boil and have a bowl of iced water on standby. Blanch the shelled peas in the boiling water for 15 seconds, then immediately refresh in the iced water. Once cool, remove the outer skin of the peas by pinching their tips and exposing the insides. Discard the skins and set the peas aside in a suitable container, keeping the pan over the heat.

Meanwhile, remove the pea custard mixture from the fridge, whisk well and season with sea salt, then divide the mixture evenly among eight ceramic dariole moulds. Cover each mould tightly with plastic wrap and place in a 90°C (195°F) steamer for 11 minutes, or until the custards are just set.

Reheat the chicken stock and brown butter mixture.

Separate out the pea leaf tips and buds, add both to the pan of boiling water and blanch for 10 seconds, then remove and leave to drain. Add the remaining pea tendrils and peas to the water and blanch for 5 seconds, then drain. Brush the blanched peas, buds, leaves and tendrils with melted butter and season lightly with salt. Spoon the custards out into individual warmed serving bowls and arrange the leaves, buds, tendrils and peas around the custards. Spoon over at least a tablespoon of the chicken stock and brown butter mixture over each dish, garnish with the pea flowers and serve.

Manganji Sweet Pepper

FAMILY

SOLANACEAE

SPECIES

CAPSICUM ANNUUM

CULTIVAR

MANGANJI

The Manganji pepper is considered to be the king of sweet peppers in Japan. Designated as *kyo yasai*, one of the forty-one specialty vegetables grown in the Kyoto region considered to have distinct qualities, it was developed in the 1920s by Japanese growers who intentionally crossed traditional Japanese fushimi peppers with Californian bell peppers. The resulting Manganji pepper, named after the temple in Maizuru city in northern Kyoto, has a thicker wall than other similar peppers and a lacquered shiny surface. It is often eaten green, although, allowed to fully ripen, the skin becomes red and the rich, sweet, fruity flavour becomes fully realised. —— Sweet peppers were originally introduced into Japan by Portuguese missionaries in the 16th century, though their origins lie in south and central America, where they are believed to have been cultivated by the indigenous populations from 7500 BC. No matter where they are grown, peppers love the sun and need a warm climate to do well. They grow best in loam or sandy soils with a wide-ranging pH (anything from pH 5–8) and need good drainage, although they also need regular moisture – too many nutrients can result in excess leaf growth and poor fruit formation. —— Each summer I attempt to grow different varieties of both sweet and hot chilli peppers. The Manganji peppers I grew this year are among my all-time favourite peppers and I quite understand why they are considered a delicacy in Japan, where they are often charcoal grilled in high-end restaurants.

CHARCOAL-ROASTED MANGANJI PEPPER
WITH BLACK GARLIC PASTE

SERVES 8

At the height of summer, when these peppers are ripe, there is nothing better than just charcoal grilling them and adorning them with this simple fermented black garlic paste.

BLACK GARLIC PASTE

50 g (1¾ oz) unsalted butter
50 g (1¾ oz) finely diced shallots
50 g (1¾ oz) inner celery stalk, white part only, finely diced
200 g (7 oz) fermented black garlic cloves, peeled
200 ml (7 fl oz) Chicken Stock (see Basics, page 240)
sea salt

Melt the butter in a saucepan, add the shallots and celery and gently sauté until translucent. Add the garlic cloves and chicken stock, increase the heat to high and simmer until almost all the liquid has evaporated. Place the contents into a food processor or blender and blitz on high speed for 1 minute. Pass through a fine-mesh sieve, season to taste with sea salt and refrigerate until needed (it will keep for up to 1 week).

Additional ingredients

16 Manganji sweet peppers
extra-virgin olive oil
sea salt

To serve

Heat a charcoal grill and, when the charcoal is glowing and the grill is quite hot, lightly brush the peppers with olive oil and sprinkle with salt. Grill the peppers until they soften and the skin starts to blister. (If you don't have a charcoal grill, a cast-iron griddle pan makes an acceptable substitute here.)

Remove the peppers from the heat, then brush again with olive oil and sprinkle with salt. Place a spoonful of the garlic paste on each serving plate, lay the peppers alongside and serve immediately.

Kohlrabi

FAMILY

BRASSICACEAE

SPECIES

BRASSICA OLERACEA VAR. **GONGYLODES**

CULTIVAR

DELICACY WHITE

Kohlrabi has enjoyed a recent popularity surge with chefs around the world. It is a member of the huge *Brassicaceae* family, meaning that, like cauliflower, cabbage, kale, broccoli and other cruciferous vegetables, it was derived from a single wild cabbage ancestor that was domesticated 2500 years ago. It is, however, a relatively recent addition to the family, having been selected just over 400 years ago; its origins lie in Northwestern Europe, where it was developed from a marrow-stem kale – a fodder crop with a thickened stem. The name itself is derived from the German *kohl* meaning cabbage and *rabi* meaning turnip; however, while kohlrabi's swollen stem resembles a turnip, the turnip is botanically a swollen root, whereas the kohlrabi is a swollen stem. —— Traditionally, kohlrabi has not been grown widely outside of northern Europe, apart from in India and southern China, where it has gained some popularity. Kohlrabi cultivars come in different shades of light green and purple, and have an unusual appearance due to the leaf-topped stems that protrude from their spherical heart. Most kohlrabies can grow to the size of a tennis ball, though those grown from autumn into winter should generally be harvested at a larger size than those grown in spring, which are best picked smaller, as the warmer weather brings on a woody texture. Kohlrabies are easy to grow and do best in full sun with well-drained, fertile soil with a pH of 6–7.5. The soil should be prepared with lots of compost and manure as, like all brassicas, kohlrabies are heavy feeders. To prevent the kohlrabi bulbs from becoming woody, they should be watered well in drier weather. —— Kohlrabi is a relatively mild-tasting member of the brassica family, appreciated for its crisp texture, and Delicacy White is a favourite cultivar of mine, which I like to grow for its pale skin and relative sweetness. It is at its best, I think, when very young and eaten raw, lending itself well as a crisp addition to salads, as well as making excellent pickles.

YOUNG KOHLRABI, SMOKED YOGHURT, ROASTED HEMP SEED

A very young kohlrabi can be as crisp as an apple. Here, it is served simply as an appetiser with smoked yoghurt and roasted hemp seed, the latter providing a wonderful nutty texture and flavour.

NOTE: *I like to lightly cold-smoke the yoghurt for this dish; it adds a subtle smokiness and depth to the flavour. The dish also works well with plain yoghurt, but if you choose to cold-smoke your yoghurt, set up a cold smoking apparatus with maple wood chips and cold-smoke your yoghurt for 20 minutes.*

16 very young Delicacy White kohlrabi (or other small green kohlrabi)
80 ml (2½ fl oz/⅓ cup) cold-pressed hemp seed oil
80 g (2¾ oz) hulled hemp seed
zest of ½ lemon
sea salt
200 g (7 oz) Greek-style strained yoghurt, regular or cold-smoked (see Note)

Bring a large saucepan of salted water to the boil and have a bowl of iced water at the ready.

Using a sharp knife or a vegetable peeler, lightly trim the base of the kohlrabi and remove some of the leaves from the stems. Blanch the kohlrabi for 20 seconds in the boiling salted water and immediately refresh in the iced water. Drain the kohlrabi and set aside.

Warm half of the hemp seed oil in a non-stick frying pan over a medium heat, add the hemp seed and cook for 2–3 minutes, stirring continuously, until lightly golden. Remove from the heat, stir in the lemon zest and season with sea salt to taste, then transfer to paper towel to drain and leave to cool.

When ready to serve, add a large spoonful of the yoghurt, smoked or otherwise, to the centre of each serving plate. Place a spoonful of the hemp seed by the side of the yoghurt, then divide the blanched kohlrabi among the plates evenly. Dress with the remaining hemp seed oil and season with sea salt.

Smooth Loofah

FAMILY

CUCURBITACEA

SPECIES

LUFFA AEGYPTIACA

P art of the large *Cucurbitacea* family, whose relatives include melon, squash, pumpkin and marrow, the loofah is a tropical and subtropical species thought to have originated either in north Africa or somewhere on the Indian subcontinent. While in the West we generally think of the loofah (sometimes spelled 'luffa'; the name having been adopted by European botanists in the 17th century from the Egyptian Arabic 'luf') as being just a long, fibrous bathroom back scrubber, when picked young it can also be a delicious, tender vegetable. Very popular in India, China and other parts of Asia, it is similar in texture to zucchini, albeit even more tender. —— Loofahs need a warm, humid climate to do well and, if grown outside the tropics, need to be planted as a summer annual where there is a long, warm summer season. The loofah fruit is borne on long, climbing vines that grow up to 10 m (30 ft) in length and which, once established, are very prolific. They are best grown on a large trellis structure and can make an impressive vertical garden if grown in this manner with the fruits hanging from the frame. The vines bear both male and female flowers – edible and delicious, these can be treated much as you would zucchini flowers. For eating, the fruits need to be picked young when they are about 30 cm (12 in) long and 4–5 cm (1 ½–2 in) in diameter; if you leave them to fully mature on the vine they will reach double this size and will be too fibrous to eat – however it is at this point that you can leave them to fully dry on the vine before peeling away the skin to expose the dried fibrous loofah we know as a bathroom exfoliator (simply shake the seeds out of the centre before use). —— In parts of Asia the loofah is known as the 'dishrag sponge' as it is used for scrubbing pots and pans, but I would urge you to try growing it as a vegetable because it is delicious and has the ability to soak up flavours especially when cooked in soups and braises. My chosen variety is the smooth loofah (*Luffa aegyptiaca*), though there is another species known as the ridged loofah or Chinese okra (*Luffa acutangula*) that is also used as a vegetable and is worth hunting down.

STEAMED LOOFAH, MUD CRAB BROTH

SERVES 8

We all know loofah as the bath sponge but in its young, fresh form it is a delightful vegetable. Similar in flavour to a zucchini, but lighter and with a spongier texture, it is excellent at absorbing other flavours. Here, it is simply steamed and served with a rich mud crab broth.

2 x 1 kg (2 lb 3 oz) live mud crabs
20 g (¾ oz/1½ tablespoons) finely sliced fresh ginger
30 g (1 oz/2 tablespoons) finely sliced spring onion (scallion), white part only
1.5 litres (51 fl oz/6 cups) Chicken Stock (see Basics, page 240)
1 fresh medium-sized smooth loofah (approx. 400 g/14 oz)
sea salt
50 ml (1¾ fl oz) melted butter

Add the mud crabs to an ice slurry and leave for 30 minutes to chill thoroughly. (Chilling the mud crabs before boiling them sends them into a semi-coma and is a more humane way of dispatching them.)

Bring a large stockpot of salted water to the boil. Add the chilled crabs to the pot and boil for 9 minutes, then remove from the pot, transfer to the refrigerator and leave to cool completely. Once cold, crack the crab shells and extract as much meat as possible (you will need at least 400 g/14 oz here). Roughly shred the meat with your fingers, checking that there are no shell fragments left and discarding any that you find. Refrigerate until needed.

Add the ginger, spring onion and chicken stock to a large saucepan and bring to the boil, then remove from the heat and leave to infuse for 30 minutes. Strain, discarding the solids, then return to the pan and keep warm over a low heat.

Peel the loofah with a vegetable peeler and cut into eight 5 cm (2 in) discs. Place the discs in a steamer basket set over simmering water and steam for 2 minutes, or until tender.

Meanwhile, add the crabmeat to the warm stock, increase the heat and bring to a simmer. Season to taste with salt.

Remove the loofah from the steamer, brush with melted butter and season with sea salt. Ladle the mud crab broth into warmed serving bowls and top with the steamed loofah discs. Serve.

Globe Artichoke

FAMILY

ASTERACEAE

SPECIES

CYNARA SCOLYMUS

CULTIVAR

VIOLET DE PROVENCE

Most likely originating in north Africa, globe artichokes have been enjoyed in the Mediterranean region since before the Ancient Greeks and Romans, with artichoke seeds having been found during excavations in Egypt during the Roman period. While the Ancient Greeks believed them to have aphrodisiac properties (and that their consumption would produce male children), today they are appreciated purely for their culinary qualities, especially in France and Italy, where, along with asparagus, they are considered to be spring delicacies. —— With relatives including lettuces, Jerusalem artichokes, thistles, sunflowers and dandelions, artichokes are sun-loving perennial plants that grow particularly well in maritime environments and regions with high rainfalls, warm climates and greater humidity. They prefer a fairly nutrient-rich soil with a pH of 5.5–6 and, during flowering, require a constant level of moisture. The artichoke globe itself is the bud of the flower and must be harvested before flowering occurs, or else the flesh will become tough and inedible. Artichoke globes come in different sizes, which vary not just from variety to variety but also depending on where on the plant they grow, with larger globes forming on the central stalk, medium globes forming on the side shoots and very small globes forming at the base of the plant. In the best growing conditions you can expect ten to twelve globes per plant. The most prized part of the artichoke is the base and inner heart. —— While the initial preparation of artichoke globes can deter some people from cooking with them at home, the most important part of the process is stripping them of their coarse outer leaves and peeling the stem and base. To keep them from oxidising during the preparation process, have a large bowl of acidulated water (a mixture of lemon juice and water) handy. Prepare the artichokes one at a time and submerge the exposed hearts in the acidulated water as you go. They are good cooked in a variety of different stocks, with many preferring vegetable-based stocks featuring wine and herbs – though whichever way you cook them, you will need to remember to remove the choke (the fine fibrous part found at the very centre of the bud) before eating. —— I love the fact that artichokes can be prepared in numerous ways and can be preserved for use throughout the year, and one of my favourite varieties is the Violet de Provence, a French heirloom that is noted for its fine flavour and strikingly beautiful purple buds.

PETER GILMORE

SALAD OF VIOLET DE PROVENCE ARTICHOKE

SERVES 8

This artichoke salad combines three textures of artichoke: a purée,
sliced hearts and fried young leaves.

PREPARED ARTICHOKE HALVES

juice of 2 lemons
16 Violet de Provence artichokes (or other purple globe
    artichokes)
4 garlic cloves, finely sliced
10 thyme sprigs
2 fresh bay leaves
10 black peppercorns, crushed
pinch of sea salt
500 ml (17 fl oz/2 cups) extra-virgin olive oil

Add half the lemon juice to a large bowl of iced water.

Cut off the stem of one of the artichokes 5 cm (2 in) from the
base. Using a sharp knife or serrated bread knife, cut the first third
off the tip of the artichoke head, then remove the tough outer
leaves with your hands to leave only the soft leaves around the
heart. Peel a couple of layers of the tough skin from the base and
stem of the artichoke using a vegetable peeler, then immediately
plunge the prepared artichoke into the lemon iced water and
submerge fully. Repeat with the remaining artichokes.

Combine the garlic, thyme, bay leaves, peppercorns, salt and
olive oil in a bowl together with the remaining lemon juice and
whisk together well, then transfer the mixture to a large vacuum-
seal bag.

Cut the prepared artichokes in half, remove the central fibrous
chokes with a sharp knife or small teaspoon, then transfer
immediately to the bag with the oil mixture and seal the bag,
removing all the air. Steam the artichoke halves in the bag on high
steam for about 20 minutes, or until tender. Leave to cool.

ARTICHOKE PURÉE, BASES AND LEAVES

1 golden shallot, finely diced
1 small inner celery stalk, white part only, finely diced
1 garlic clove, finely diced
30 g (1 oz) unsalted butter
250 ml (8½ fl oz/1 cup) Chicken Stock (see Basics, page 240)
Prepared Artichoke Halves (see left)
sea salt
50 g (1¾ oz) crème fraîche

In a small saucepan, sauté the shallot, celery and garlic in the
butter until translucent. Add the chicken stock to the pan, remove
from the heat and set aside.

Open the vacuum-seal bag containing the prepared artichoke
halves and divide the oil within equally between two separate
containers. Cut all the leaves off the artichokes and add the leaves
to one of the containers, adding extra oil if necessary to ensure
they are fully submerged. Submerge 16 of the artichoke halves
in the oil in the other container, adding more oil as necessary.
Set both containers aside.

Add the remaining artichoke halves to the saucepan with the
chicken stock, bring to a simmer and cook over a high heat for
5–8 minutes, until virtually all the stock has evaporated and the
artichoke hearts are soft. Remove the pan from the heat, transfer
the contents to a food processor and blitz together until smooth,
then pass the contents through a fine-mesh sieve and leave to
cool completely. Once cool, season with sea salt to taste and
fold through the crème fraîche. Refrigerate until needed.

Additional ingredients

1 litre (34 fl oz/4 cups) sunflower oil
sea salt
160 g (5½ oz) goat's milk feta
about 20 kailan flower petals (optional)

To serve

In a large heavy-based saucepan, heat the sunflower oil to 180°C
(350°F). Drain the oil-submerged artichoke leaves and pat dry with
paper towel, then add to the pan with the hot oil in small batches
and deep-fry for 1–2 minutes until golden brown. Drain well on
paper towel and season with sea salt.

Drain the oil-submerged artichoke halves and pat dry with
paper towel, then cut into thin slices. Season with sea salt.

Spread a tablespoon of the artichoke purée across the centre of
each serving plate, top with the artichoke slices and crumble over
the feta. Pile a small stack of the fried artichoke leaves over the top
and garnish with kalian flower petals, if using.

Japanese Red Turnip

FAMILY
BRASSICACEAE

SPECIES
BRASSICA RAPA* VAR. *RAPIFERA

CULTIVAR
HIDA BENI

The turnip (or 'kabu' in Japan) is one of the oldest vegetables to be cultivated and is said to have made its way to Japan via China and Afghanistan – a journey that must have taken place around the 8th or 9th century, as references can be found to the turnip in ancient Japanese chronicles from this time. In the centuries that followed more than eighty varieties of kabu evolved with varying colours, shapes and tastes, with most of these, including the red-skinned varieties that were grown in mountainous regions, being developed in isolation. This level of diversity is not seen in any other country and is what has elevated the kabu to be regarded as an iconic vegetable in Japan alongside the daikon (Japanese radish), also of the *Brassicaceae* family. ——— The Hida Beni red turnip is a scarlet-skinned, flattened globe-shaped turnip cultivated mainly in Japan's Takayama city and surrounds. It originated in the city's Nyukawa area – a part of the city once named Hachigago and known as the place where the round, reddish-purple turnips, or 'Hachiga kabu', were grown. It was in among these turnips in 1918 that a red-coloured mutant was discovered, which later came to be called 'Hida Beni kabu' or 'the red turnip of Hida', the 'beni' referring to a particular shade of red that comes from the pigment of the 'benibana' (safflower) that has been used to paint the inside of sake cups and small plates since ancient times. ——— Unlike its vivid red skin, Hida Beni's flesh is white with some internal red streaking. It has a mild, sweet flavour and, like other Japanese turnips, can be eaten raw in salads. Traditionally, however, it is pickled and, during this process, the red pigments leach from the skin, staining the white flesh red and resulting in a vibrant, naturally coloured pickle that is celebrated for its beautiful red hue. ——— Hida Beni, like all Japanese turnips, is best grown in cool-climate conditions. It is best grown fast and picked young, especially if planted in spring.

HIDA BENI RED TURNIP PICKLES

MAKES 1 X 500 ML (17 FL OZ/2 CUP) JAR

The heirloom Hida Beni red turnip from Japan makes excellent rose-coloured pickles, which are perfect for snacking on on their own or for accompanying sushi and sashimi. Ume mirin is mirin that has been infused with a preserved Japanese plum; you can use regular mirin if it's unavailable.

4 medium-sized Hida Beni red turnips
20 g (¾ oz) sea salt
200 ml (7 fl oz) rice vinegar
50 g (1¾ oz) caster (superfine) sugar
100 ml (3½ fl oz) ume mirin or regular mirin

Peel the turnips and cut them crossways into 2 mm (⅛ in) slices using a mandoline or a sharp knife.

Spread the turnip slices out in a shallow dish and sprinkle over the sea salt. Leave for 1 hour, or until the turnip slices have bled some juice and become pliable, then squeeze them dry with your hands and place in a sterilised jar.

Combine the rice vinegar, sugar and mirin in a bowl and stir until the sugar has dissolved. Pour the pickling mixture over the turnips to fill the jar as close to the top as possible, then screw on the cap and shake the jar well. Transfer to the refrigerator and leave for a few days before using (the pickles will keep, refrigerated, for 2–3 months).

Redmeat Radish (Watermelon Radish)

FAMILY
BRASSICACEAE

SPECIES
RAPHANUS SATIVUS

CULTIVAR
BEAUTY HEART

For anyone wanting to start a vegetable garden for the first time, radishes should be high on the list. They germinate quickly (within three to four days) and some varieties can be enjoyed within as little as three weeks – as far as instant gratification goes, these are about as good as it gets. —— There is a lot of conjecture surrounding the origins of the radish's domestication, with some scientists believing them to have been selected from a wild plant *R. raphanistrum* found in the eastern Mediterranean and others believing that the only true wild forms to have been discovered are Southeast Asian in origin. Though many sources cite that the Egyptians were growing radishes as early as 2000 BC, it is also widely accepted that many of the varieties that we enjoy today were cultivated in China around 500 BC. The species name *Raphanus* derives from the Greek 'ra' meaning 'quickly' and 'phainomai' meaning 'to appear', in reference to its rapid germination, while the common name 'radish' is derived from the Latin for root, 'radix'. —— Radishes come in a large variety of colours – pink, red, purple, yellow, green and black – though their flesh is generally white. Some of the most impressive forms of radish were originally developed in China and include the daikon and mooli, although the Japanese Sakurajima radish is probably the most impressive of all and can grow up to about 40 kg (110 lb), roughly the size of a large pumpkin. These larger Asian radishes are often pickled or slowly braised and eaten as a vegetable, while most small European-style radishes, such as the French Breakfast or the Cherrybell, are generally eaten raw in salads. Young radish leaves and immature seed pods are also edible. —— Radishes prefer full sun in light sandy loam soils with a pH of 6.5–7. Probably because their pungent odour deters insects and pests such as aphids and cucumber beetles, radishes are useful companion plants for many other crops; they function as a trap crop luring insects away from the main crop. Cucumbers and radishes seem to thrive when grown together, while radishes also grow well with lettuces and peas. —— The redmeat radish – a stunning radish that grows to about the size of a baseball and has bright pink flesh – was developed in China and is also known as the watermelon radish. It is one of the first vegetables I grew at home more than ten years ago and then introduced to Quay restaurant through one of my original growers in the Blue Mountains. These radishes take ten to twelve weeks to mature, prefer a slightly more clay loam soil (in keeping with some other late-season crops) and are best sown in autumn – the deep pink-to-red colour develops best when night temperatures fall to about 10°C (50°F). When I first grew these radishes, they were pretty much unheard of in Australia, and certainly weren't available commercially. Unusual radishes and coloured carrots were some of the first heirloom vegetables I introduced onto my menus that gained attention from customers and fellow chefs. It is gratifying to see that some of these vegetables are now more widely available.

TARTARE OF WAGYU, FERMENTED CHILLI, REDMEAT RADISHES

In this dish the pairing of a spicy, dressed tartare of beef with the crisp redmeat radish delivers real textural impact, while the cooling effect of the crème fraîche tempers the heat of the fermented chilli and radishes to produce an intense – but well integrated – flavour combination. An optional garnish of fresh marshmallow flowers, from the ancient herb that inspired the confection of the same name, adds a delicate touch to what is an essentially rustic dish.

FERMENTED CHILLI AND MISO PASTE

100 g (3½ oz) gochujang (Korean fermented red chilli paste)
100 g (3½ oz) yellow miso paste
2 teaspoons virgin black sesame oil
2 teaspoons Garlic-infused Oil (see Basics, page 241)
50 g (1¾ oz) softened unsalted butter

Combine all the ingredients in a bowl and whisk together well. Pass the mixture through a fine-mesh sieve and set aside at room temperature until needed.

MILK SKIN (OPTIONAL GARNISH)

500 ml (17 fl oz/2 cups) milk

Add the milk to a large wide saucepan or frying pan and bring just to boiling point, then remove then pan from the heat and leave the milk to cool and form a skin. Using your fingers and working from the edge of the pan, carefully remove the milk skin from the milk and lay it on an oiled sheet of non-stick baking paper. Return the saucepan to the heat and repeat this process a second time. Transfer the baking paper sheet with the milk skins on it to a dehydrator or a very low oven preheated to 50°C (120°F) and dehydrate until crisp, about 1–2 hours. Once crisp, break the skin into shards and place in a sealed airtight container until required.

Additional ingredients

700 g (1 lb 9 oz) wagyu beef rump, well trimmed
8 redmeat radishes, leaves trimmed and reserved
50 ml (1¾ fl oz) extra-virgin olive oil
sea salt
200 g (7 oz) crème fraîche
about 20 marshmallow flowers or other edible
    white flowers (optional)

To serve

Using a sharp knife, cut the wagyu rump into 5 mm (¼ in) cubes. Transfer to a bowl and set aside to come to room temperature.

Peel the radishes and cut into 3 mm (⅛ in) thin slices, then punch out a disc from each slice using a 2.5 cm (1 in) round cutter. Place the radish discs into a bowl, dress with the extra-virgin olive oil and season with sea salt.

Dress the wagyu beef with the chilli miso paste and mix together well. Divide the dressed beef evenly among serving plates, topping each with a spoonful of crème fraîche, then scatter over the radish discs and garnish with the radish leaves and the milk skin shards and marshmallow flowers, if using. Serve.

Sacred Lotus

FAMILY

NELUMBONACEAE

SPECIES

NELUMBO NUCIFERA

CULTIVAR

JADE GREEN

The symbolism, mythology and religious beliefs that surround the lotus are numerous. The national flower of India, and sacred to both Hindus and Buddhists, it is seen as an example of divine beauty, with its unfolding petals suggesting the expansion of the soul. Botanically speaking, the sacred lotus is also an astonishing plant. Researchers have found that it has the remarkable ability to regulate the temperature of its flowers to within a narrow range just as humans and other warm-blooded animals do; physiologists at the University of Adelaide found that lotus flowers blooming in the Adelaide Botanical Gardens managed to maintain a temperature of 30–35°C (85–95°F) even when the air temperature dropped to 10°C (50°F) in what they believe to be an attempt to attract cold-blooded insect pollinators. Remarkably, lotus seeds also remain viable for many years, with the oldest recorded lotus seed germination being from a 1300-year-old seed recovered from a dry lakebed in north-eastern China. —— Native to tropical Asia and northern Australia, sacred lotus is an aquatic perennial that requires temperatures of above 24°C (75°F) in summer to do well. The roots of the lotus are generally planted in the soil of a pond or riverbed (though they can also be grown in pots or containers submerged in water and are often grown as part of water features), while the leaves float on the top of the water surface or are held above it. The lotus can grow to a height of about 1.5 m (5 ft), with the leaves as large as 60 cm (24 in) in diameter and the flowers, which are found on the thick stems rising several centimetres above the leaves, being up to 20 cm (8 in) in diameter. The pods form after the flowers die back and contain the fresh seed. —— All parts of the lotus plant are edible but it is mostly grown for its rhizomes and seeds. Cultivars are generally divided into three categories: lotus grown for its rhizomes, lotus grown for its seeds and lotus grown for its flowers. Seventy per cent of lotus grown for human consumption is produced in China, where it is estimated that 740,000 acres of land is devoted to lotus production. The most widely used system is crop rotation with rice and vegetables: the lotus rhizome is planted early in the year and harvested in July, after which rice can be planted into the same field followed by vegetables such as cabbage or spinach. Alternatively, lotus can be grown year-round in ponds that are used to raise aquatic animals such as freshwater fish and shrimp, an efficient use of water resources for both. —— While the lotus rhizomes are an interesting starchy vegetable that is often thinly sliced and fried, for me it is the fresh lotus seeds that are the real prize. Most lotus seeds are available in their dried form; they are either boiled and used in soups or congees or, most typically, turned into a paste that is widely used in Chinese pastries and Japanese desserts. However, the seeds I source are freshly harvested in the Northern Territory of Australia and are available for only a short period of the year, about four weeks. Peeling the outer green shell exposes their soft white inner seed, which is delicious eaten raw or quickly stir-fried.

PETER GILMORE

FRESH LOTUS SEEDS, GINGER CHAWANMUSHI, WAKAME BROTH

SERVES 8

Fresh lotus seeds are a rare seasonal treat, harvested in summer in the subtropics. Once their green shells are removed, the seeds in their fresh form are tender yet crisp in texture, similar to an immature nut but with a flavour reminiscent of young corn. Here, I have blanched them simply in boiling water and served them with a ginger *chawanmushi* (savoury custard).

WAKAME BROTH

30 g (1 oz) dried shiitake mushrooms
20 g (¾ oz) dried wakame seaweed
1.5 litres (51 fl oz/6 cups) Chicken Stock (see Basics, page 240)
sea salt

Add the dried shiitake mushrooms and wakame to a large saucepan, pour over the chicken stock and bring almost to the boil, then turn the heat to very low and leave to simmer very gently for 1 hour, or until reduced by about two-thirds. Strain the broth through a fine-mesh sieve, season to taste with salt and refrigerate until needed (it will keep for 2–3 days).

SCHMALTZ

100 g (3½ oz) chicken fat, finely chopped
1 tablespoon water
sea salt

Add the chicken fat and water to a small saucepan set over a low heat. Leave until the fat has rendered completely, then remove from the heat and pour the liquid fat through a fine-mesh sieve. Season to taste with salt, transfer to a suitable container and refrigerate until needed (it will keep for 4–5 days), reheating it gently to return it to a liquid before use.

GINGER CHAWANMUSHI

50 g (1¾ oz) finely sliced fresh ginger
1 garlic clove, finely sliced
2 tablespoons finely sliced spring onion (scallion), white part only
750 ml (25½ fl oz/3 cups) Chicken Stock (see Basics, page 240)
5 eggs
sea salt

Add the ginger, garlic and spring onion to a saucepan together with the chicken stock and bring to the boil. Reduce the heat and simmer gently for 3 minutes, then remove from the heat and leave to infuse for 30 minutes. Strain and leave to cool completely.

Once cool, measure out 600 ml (20½ fl oz) of the infused stock into a bowl, add the eggs and whisk together well. Season to taste with salt, then divide the mixture evenly among eight 175 ml (6 fl oz) ceramic dariole moulds or ramekins. Cover each tightly with plastic wrap and place in an 80°C (175°F) steamer for 13–15 minutes, or until the custard is just set.

Additional ingredients

about 100 shelled lotus seeds, three-quarters halved and the remainder left whole
16 young barletta onions or pearl onions, halved
8 garlic chive buds
12 sour Mexican cucumbers, halved widthways (optional)
50 ml (1¾ fl oz) melted butter
sea salt

To serve

Melt the schmaltz and heat the wakame broth in separate saucepans.

Blanch the lotus seeds (both halved and whole) and onions in a large saucepan of salted water for 1 minute. Add the garlic chives and Mexican sour cucumbers and blanch for a further 10 seconds, then strain all the vegetables. Dress the vegetables in the melted butter and season with sea salt.

Spoon the custards out into individual serving bowls and top with the dressed vegetables. Spoon 2 tablespoons of the hot wakame broth over each bowl and finish each with a drizzle of the melted schmaltz. Serve.

JERE GETTLE

When I first started growing vegetables in my own garden I quickly realised that I was entering a whole new world of diversity, and that what was available in the local marketplace was only a fraction of the variety of vegetables you could grow. I started to research seed companies from all over the world, spending hours in front of a computer screen looking at online catalogues. Within Australia I searched Diggers and Eden, among others, for seeds, but further afield I also searched Italian, French, English and Irish seed companies too (with Seedaholic in Ireland being one of my favourites). However, of all the countries in the world I found the greatest diversity of heirloom and rare seeds to be in the United States.

Being the home of mass production, fast food and genetically engineered food, this was contrary to what I believed the US food system to be about, however the US also has an incredible grassroots movement of organic farming and heirloom seed-saving networks. As a result, my most valued resources for seeds are companies like Wild Garden Seeds, Gourmet Seeds, Restoration Seeds and the Kitazawa Seed Company – though Baker Creek Heirloom Seeds, based in Mansfield, Missouri, is the most inspiring and fruitful of the lot.

In 2016 I visited Jere Gettle there at his farm and experienced one of the most inspiring days talking with him about his approach, walking through his extensive farm and observing his own private seed bank. Without a doubt, Baker Creek has the biggest variety of rare and heirloom seeds commercially available, maintaining as they do more than 2000 varieties of non-hybrid, non-GMO, open-pollinated seeds. I source a lot of the seeds that my network of growers grow for the restaurants from Baker Creek, though I first grow these new varieties in my home test garden to make sure they have the flavour and qualities I'm looking for. Australia has quite tough quarantine laws for the importation of seeds. Over the years, some seeds have been allowed to be imported and some have not. The rules seem to change every couple of years, but I have managed to save a lot of varieties that are no longer able to be imported.

In 2011, Jere initiated a National Heirloom Expo, which is now held in Santa Rosa, California in September each year. I visited the Expo in 2017 and I felt like a kid in a candy store. Seed companies, farmers and growers from all over the country come together to show off their produce, exchange information and take part in seminars. The size of the natural food movement in the US is enormous and inspiring.

Here, Jere explains how he started Baker Creek Heirloom Seeds –

I always had an interest in seeds since I planted my first seeds in the family garden when I was three years old. I loved to sit and look at seed catalogues. My interest in saving seeds came about when I realised as a child that some of my favourite things were disappearing from the catalogues. That led to my wanting to save varieties from disappearing. When I was twelve years old, my family moved to Missouri, where we had a longer growing season. By that time, my interest in saving seeds had grown into a real hobby.

I was always interested in history of all kinds, but became particularly interested in the history of seeds. I loved to find varieties of seeds that had a fascinating history and that had been handed down from generation to generation – seeds that were rare and not available everywhere. I loved growing unusual things and saving the seeds. As I continued to grow and save seeds, I collected so many that I needed to start doing something with them. I began packaging them and selling them at local swap meets and the like, but my accumulation of seeds continued to grow. My hobby had turned into a business. In 1997, when I was seventeen years old, I published my first seed catalogue and began offering seeds commercially. My business really took off in the year 2000 when people worried that the turn of the century would bring about a shortage of food. The 'Y2K' scare made people begin planting their own gardens and saving seeds.

Baker Creek Heirloom Seeds is named after the little creek that runs through the farm property. The company began with my interest in saving seed varieties and that interest heads the goal of the company today, which is to save and protect plant diversity and food purity. We try to find obscure and rare seeds, to make them available for others to grow and to keep them in circulation. Saving heirloom plant varieties helps to ensure that we will have a safer food supply for future generations.

Recommended Seed Companies

Baker Creek Heirloom Seeds
rareseeds.com
seeds@rareseeds.com
+ 1 417 924 8917

2278 Baker Creek Road
Mansfield, Missouri 65704
USA

The Diggers Club
diggers.com.au
+ 61 3 5984 7900

PO Box 300
Dromana, Victoria 3936
Australia

Gourmet Seed
gourmetseed.com
+ 1 831 637 2411
customerservice@gourmetseed.com

743 Shore Road
Hollister, California 95023
USA

Green Seed Tasmania
greenseedtas.com.au
mail@greenseedtas.com

GPO Box 735
Hobart, Tasmania 7001
Australia

Kitazawa Seed Company
kitazawaseed.com
seeds@kitazawaseed.com
+ 1 510 595-1188

201 4th Street
Oakland, California 94607
USA

Restoration Seeds
restorationseeds.com
service@restorationseeds.com

9969 Wagner Creek Road
Talent, Oregon 97540
USA

Seedaholic
seedaholic.com
orders@seedaholic.com
+ 353 94 954 8756

Cloghbrack, Clonbur, Galway
Ireland

Wild Garden Seeds
wildgardenseed.com
karen@wildgardenseed.com
+ 1 541 929-4068

PO Box 1509
Philomath, Oregon 97370
USA

Basics

UMAMI STOCK

MAKES APPROX. 1.5 LITRES (51 FL OZ/6 CUPS)

1 snapper head or other fish head, halved
   (ask your fishmonger to do this for you)
50 ml (1¾ fl oz) grapeseed oil
1 kg (2 lb 3 oz) chicken wings, roughly chopped
250 g (9 oz) squid trimmings
250 g (9 oz) scallop trimmings or small scallops
2 small fennel bulbs, diced
2 inner celery stalks, white parts only, diced
½ brown onion, diced
125 g (4½ oz) unsalted butter
1 garlic clove, diced
100 ml (3½ fl oz) good-quality apple-cider vinegar
375 ml (12½ fl oz/1½ cups) dry unoaked chardonnay
1.5 litres (51 fl oz/6 cups) Chicken Stock (see right)
1 litre (34 fl oz/4 cups) water
500 g (1 lb 2 oz) pippies (vongole) or other clams,
   shells well scrubbed

Remove and discard the eyes and gills from the halved snapper head, then wash thoroughly under running water to remove the excess blood.

Heat the oil in a stockpot over a medium–high heat, add the snapper head and cook, turning occasionally, for 5 minutes, or until lightly golden all over. Add the chicken wings, squid and scallop trimmings and cook for 2 minutes until everything is well coloured, then add the fennel, celery, onion and butter and continue to cook, stirring and scraping the base of the pot as you go to prevent the ingredients from sticking, until the vegetables are softened and golden brown. Add the garlic and apple-cider vinegar and cook, stirring and scraping well so that all of the brown bits on the bottom of the pot are dissolved, until almost all of the vinegar has evaporated. Pour in the wine and continue to cook until almost all of the wine has evaporated, then add the chicken stock and water. Bring to a simmer and leave to cook over a low heat for 2 hours.

After 2 hours, add the clams to the stock, remove the pot from the heat and leave the stock to infuse for 30 minutes, then strain through a fine-mesh sieve into a bowl, discarding the solids. Skim off any fat from the surface of the stock with a small ladle, then strain again through a sieve lined with muslin (cheesecloth) into a clean stockpot or very large saucepan and leave to cool. The stock will keep in the refrigerator in a suitable container for up to 4 days.

CHICKEN STOCK

MAKES 2.5 LITRES (85 FL OZ/10 CUPS)

2.5 kg (5½ lb) chicken bones
1 large brown onion, chopped
2 carrots, chopped
2 inner celery stalks, white parts only, chopped
50 ml (1¾ fl oz) grapeseed oil
4 litres (135 fl oz/16 cups) cold water

Wash the chicken bones under cold running water to remove any excess blood, then drain and set aside.

In a large heavy-based saucepan, sauté the vegetables in the grapeseed oil over a medium heat until softened. Add the drained chicken bones and sauté for 3–4 minutes, being careful not to add too much colour, then pour over the water. Bring to the boil, then reduce the heat to a very gentle simmer. Skim the stock with a ladle and leave to simmer for 4 hours (it should be just ticking over during this time). After 4 hours, skim again and strain through a fine conical strainer lined with muslin (cheesecloth), then leave to cool completely. Transfer to an airtight container and refrigerate until needed (it will keep for 2–3 days).

VEGETABLE STOCK

MAKES 1 LITRE (34 FL OZ/4 CUPS)

2 carrots, finely diced
½ fennel bulb, finely diced
1 brown onion, finely diced
1 leek, finely diced
4 inner celery stalks, white parts only, finely diced
1 garlic clove, finely diced
2 tablespoons grapeseed oil
200 ml (7 fl oz) aromatic white wine
1.2 litres (41 fl oz) cold water
5 thyme sprigs
10 parsley stalks
10 chervil sprigs
1 bay leaf
5 peppercorns, crushed

In a large heavy-based saucepan, sauté the vegetables in the grapeseed oil over a medium heat until softened but not coloured. Deglaze the pan with the wine and continue to cook until almost all the wine has evaporated, then add the water, herbs and peppercorns and bring to a very gentle simmer. Leave to simmer gently over a low heat for 30 minutes, then remove from the pan and set aside for 30 minutes to cool and to allow the flavours to infuse. Strain the stock through a fine conical strainer lined with muslin (cheesecloth), transfer to a suitable airtight container and refrigerate until needed (it will keep for 4–5 days).

SMOKED EGGPLANT CREAM

MAKES 500 G (1 LB 2 OZ)

500 ml (17 fl oz/2 cups) smoked grapeseed oil
juice of ¼ lemon
2 garlic cloves, 1 whole, 1 finely sliced
2 small firm eggplants
sea salt

Add the smoked grapeseed oil to a vacuum-seal bag together with the lemon juice and sliced garlic clove. Seal the bag, removing all the air, and cook in a steamer at 50°C (120°F) for 30 minutes. Leave the oil to cool in the bag for 10 minutes, then open and strain through an oil filter bag or muslin (cheesecloth). Discard the solids and return the oil to the bag.

One at a time, peel the eggplants and cut into 2 cm (¾ in) cubes, discarding any coloured seedy parts (when choosing the eggplant, freshness is imperative – the seeds should be very small and have not turned black inside the eggplant). Submerge the eggplant cubes in the oil before they have a chance to oxidise, then reseal the bag and steam at 95°C (205°F) for 40 minutes, or until the eggplant is soft. Strain the eggplant, reserving some of the oil, then transfer the eggplant to a blender and purée, adding a little of the oil if you need to obtain a smooth consistency. Pass through a fine drum sieve. Season with sea salt and allow to cool, then transfer to a suitable container and refrigerate until needed (it will keep for up to 5 days).

BROWN BUTTER

MAKES APPROX. 175 ML (6 FL OZ)

250 g (9 oz) unsalted butter

Add the butter to a heavy-based, high-sided saucepan and place over a high heat. Once the butter has melted and foamed, and the foam starts to turn golden-brown, carefully pour the brown butter into a large stainless-steel bowl, leaving behind as many solids as possible. Use a small ladle to remove any remaining foam from the top of the butter, which should now be golden and smell of roasted nuts. Once the surface is completely clear of impurities, ladle out the butter into a clean container, being careful not to disturb the milk solids that will remain on the bottom of the pan. Set aside to cool and refrigerate until needed (it will keep for 2–3 weeks).

GARLIC-INFUSED OIL

MAKES 250 ML (8½ FL OZ/1 CUP)

150 ml (5 fl oz) olive oil
100 ml (3½ fl oz) grapeseed oil
6 garlic cloves, finely sliced

Combine the oils in a saucepan and warm to 50°C (120°F). Add the garlic, remove the pan from the heat and leave to infuse for 2 hours. Strain.

AÏOLI

MAKES 325 ML (11 FL OZ)

4 egg yolks
1 teaspoon lemon juice
1 x Garlic-infused Oil (see above), at room temperature
1 teaspoon water
sea salt

Add the egg yolks and lemon juice to a bowl or small food processor. Add the garlic-infused oil in a slow, steady stream, whisking or processing as you go, until all the oil has been used and is fully incorporated into the egg yolks. Stir in the water to thin out the mixture and season with sea salt to taste. Refrigerate until needed (it will keep for 4–5 days).

INDEX

ACKNOWLEDGEMENTS

First and foremost, I would like to thank my wife, Kathryn Gilmore, who has been on this year-long journey with me in the writing of this book. Kath has been my researcher and scribe, spending countless hours researching each featured vegetable, referencing and cross-referencing information on species, origin and history. Without Kath, this book would not have been written. Thank you for everything, my love. On this journey there were three books we referred to regularly and I can highly recommend them for further reading: *Discovering Vegetables, Herbs and Spices* by Susanna Lyle, *Vegetable Literacy* by Deborah Madison and *The Organic Salad Garden* by Joy Larkcom.

I would like to thank the team at Hardie Grant, who have given me all the support and time necessary to produce this book. A special thank you to Jane Willson, who really believed in this book from the very beginning. Jane was in the audience at the Opera House when I gave a talk at René Redzepi's MAD Sydney conference. I spoke about my passion for growing heirloom vegetables and working closely with farmers to grow these vegetables for Quay and Bennelong. Jane approached me after the talk and said she would love to publish a book on my experience of growing heirloom vegetables. My response to her was, 'Funny you should mention this, I was already thinking this should be the subject of my next book'. It's serendipitous how small moments in time can align. The whole team at Hardie Grant have been so good to work with. Loran McDougall and Simon Davis, thank you for your professionalism, skill and hard work. A big thank you to Daniel New for his passion and skill working on the design of this book; thank you for your willingness to work so collaboratively with me. I would especially like to thank Brett Stevens for his brilliant technical ability in photographing this book. Brett was also the photographer on my second book, *Organum*. With his perfectionism and attention to detail I couldn't imagine a more professional and passionate photographer to work with. Thanks also to Paul Davies for supplying the majority of the ceramic surfaces used to shoot the food. I would also like to thank Leon Fink and the Fink family for all their support and encouragement over the years, not to mention my friends and colleagues at Quay and Bennelong restaurants.

Finally, I would like to thank all the growers featured in this book for their commitment and passion for growing beautiful vegetables in a way that is kind to the earth, and for their generosity in sharing their knowledge in this book.

ABOUT THE AUTHOR

Peter Gilmore is the executive chef at two of Australia's most exciting and dynamic restaurants: Bennelong at the Sydney Opera House and Quay Restaurant across the harbour in The Rocks.

Peter was inspired to cook at a young age and started his apprenticeship at sixteen, then spent his twenties developing his own style in kitchens overseas and in country New South Wales.

Peter is now one of the most awarded chefs in Australia. For an unprecedented sixteen consecutive years, Quay was awarded three chef's hats, as well as three stars in the national *Australian Gourmet Traveller Restaurant Guide*. Quay was named Restaurant of the Year six times in the *Sydney Morning Herald Good Food Guide*, and listed for five years on the World's 50 Best Restaurants list; it also held the title of Best Restaurant in Australasia for three of those years. Bennelong took out the 'Best New Restaurant' title at all three major Australian restaurant awards when it reopened in 2015.

Peter and his cuisine are held in the highest regard within Australia and around the world. Peter is regularly invited to attend international festivals and seminars. He is proud to be an ambassador for Tourism Australia, working in pivotal roles for the Restaurant Australia campaign.

Published in 2018 by Hardie Grant Books, an imprint of Hardie Grant Publishing

Hardie Grant Books (Melbourne)
Building 1, 658 Church Street
Richmond, Victoria 3121

Hardie Grant Books (London)
5th & 6th Floors
52–54 Southwark Street
London SE1 1UN

hardiegrantbooks.com

Illustrations
Susannah Blaxill, Eggplant Number 2, charcoal, 1000 mm x 785 mm © the artist/Copyright Agency 2018
Susannah Blaxill, Brown Onion, charcoal, 810 mm x 610 mm © the artist/Copyright Agency 2018
Susannah Blaxill, Tied Beans, charcoal, 490 mm x 900 mm © the artist/Copyright Agency 2018
Susannah Blaxill, Garlic, watercolour and gouache, 160 mm x 145 mm © the artist/Copyright Agency 2018

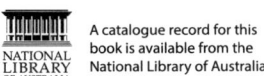 A catalogue record for this
book is available from the
NATIONAL LIBRARY OF AUSTRALIA · National Library of Australia

From the Earth
ISBN 978 1 74379 348 0

10 9 8 7 6 5 4 3 2 1

Publishing Director: Jane Willson
Researcher: Kathryn Gilmore
Managing Editor: Marg Bowman
Project Editor: Loran McDougall
Editor: Simon Davis
Design Manager: Jessica Lowe
Designer: Daniel New
Photographer: Brett Stevens
Production Manager: Todd Rechner
Production Coordinator: Tessa Spring

Colour reproduction by Splitting Image Colour Studio
Printed in China by 1010 Printing International Limited